THE CUBAN SPEECH

The United States Goes to War with Spain, 1898

WAYNE SOINI

iUniverse LLC
Bloomington

THE CUBAN SPEECH
THE UNITED STATES GOES TO WAR WITH SPAIN, 1898

iUniverse books may be ordered through booksellers or by contacting:

iUniverse
1663 Liberty Drive
Bloomington, IN 47403
www.iuniverse.com
1-800-Authors (1-800-288-4677)

ISBN: 978-1-4917-1216-0 (sc)
ISBN: 978-1-4917-1215-3 (hc)
ISBN: 978-1-4917-1214-6 (e)

Library of Congress Control Number: 2013918980

Printed in the United States of America.

iUniverse rev. date: 11/06/2013

Dedication

I DEDICATE THIS BOOK TO my late parents, Waino and Florence Soini, and to my sister, Sheila Soini Normansell. Fairness to them required me to write the most accurate, best history that I could.

Acknowledgements

I CANNOT FAIRLY ACKNOWLEDGE ALL of my debts but thanks especially to the University of Massachusetts Boston's Healey Library; its ILIAD network; the Massachusetts Historical Society; the Boston Public Library, Rare Books Room; Karl Ash, Archivist, William McKinley Presidential Library and Museum; Jennifer Barthovde, Manuscript Division, Library of Congress; Marjorie Strong, Assistant Librarian, Vermont Historical Society; and Mary Brough, Librarian, Proctor Free Library, Proctor, Vermont.

Contents

Introduction

LIKE THE JAPANESE ATTACK ON Pearl Harbor, which to this day masks many other causes of World War II, an explosion that lit up the Havana night sky in February, 1898, when the battleship *Maine* sank, killing 266 men, for a long time obscured any other causes of the War of 1898. But the once-substantial "Remember the *Maine*!" majority of historians who opined that the reign of Spain fell plainly because of the *Maine* has been displaced. A consensus of modern scholars understands that it was not a bomb on a battleship but a speech in the Senate that triggered our War of 1898. Revisionist scholars best exemplified by one of the first, Professor Gerald Linderman, have carried the day. In 1976 revisionists were heavily reinforced by the Navy when its Naval History Division published a state-of-the-art scientific study concluding that the *Maine* self-detonated.[1] Any *Maine*-biased counter-revisionists today must deal with the spooky specter of war begun by mistake.

Nothing so strange hinders focusing on Senator Redfield Proctor's late winter trip to Cuba and his subsequent words in Washington as a tipping point of history. Delivered in the Senate chamber of the Capitol on March 17, 1898, instantly known nationally, Proctor's speech was that decade's single most important address by any person on any subject. Curiously, his address was quiet and conversational. Proctor reached for no high notes, flailed with no gestures, roared no rhetoric, and

[1] H.G. Rickover, How the Battleship *Maine* was Destroyed, (Washington, D.C.: Naval History Division, Department of the Navy, 1976).

provided no quotable or dramatic lines or slogans. Nonetheless, nobody in the country proved immune to Proctor. The tide of public opinion turned as those who hoped to avoid war, reading Proctor's words, concluded that peace with Spain was shameful to maintain any longer. President William McKinley was soon moved to match Proctor's recitation; however, without his own personal observations of Cuban suffering, McKinley did so by releasing horrific dispatches from five American consuls there. The "Cuban Correspondences," as they were called, went from the State Department to every major newspaper on April 11, 1898, the same day McKinley's written message went to Congress, a message that was just as objective and factual as Proctor's. Thus, following two extended expressions of sober judgment and close analysis, combined with unofficial and official witnesses' observations of widespread Spanish inhumanity to Cubans, first by Proctor and then by McKinley, the country was aroused and Congress was led to declare war on Spain on April 25, 1898.

It need not have been so. The United States had long witnessed Cuban calamities without intervening. José Marti's anti-colonial rebellion of 1895 was only the latest of seven uprisings in Cuba during the nineteenth century. After Marti died gallantly astride a white horse leading one of his revolt's earliest, daring but ill-advised frontal charges, his revolt retracted into sporadic guerrilla war conducted all over Cuba. The rebels took no coastal cities while Spain, by Draconian methods, managed to control four of Cuba's six provinces. It seemed equally possible that the rebels and the Spaniards would fight indefinitely (Proctor's view) or that the rebels had already lost (John Tone's view) or that Spain was doomed (most Cuban scholars' view). Accordingly, one quite justifiably asks: Why, especially at this very confusing point militarily, did the United States finally decide to intervene?

Proctor is the best one-word answer to that question. It was then, and remains now, an unexpected answer. In February, 1898, several coincidences led Senator Redfield Proctor to Cuba. By extending his winter holiday in Florida a bit, Proctor originally intended a short visit to Havana, just long enough to understand business conditions on the island. Congress was in session; important legislation was under active consideration and he had to get back to Washington. Once in Havana, however, hailed by his old friend Clara Barton, Proctor found an invitation that he join her irresistible. By that chance, touring four of Cuba's six provinces with the Red Cross, Proctor unexpectedly and quickly became one of the best-informed persons on the planet on the condition of Cuban civilians. He had facts that he wanted to share. On the boat and long train ride back to Washington, Proctor made handwritten notes to be typed up as a press release. But that plan changed, too. Proctor's notes, via another series of coincidences in Washington, became an oral report. Proctor, a reticent public figure who rarely spoke, nonetheless on March 17, 1898 held forth in the Senate chamber with a first-person account on the hottest question of his time. Unlike many in Congress whom the so-called "Cuban Junto" had lobbied successfully, being entirely unaffiliated with Cuba Libré, Proctor appeared to have no agenda of his own. Taken as credible on its face by one just returned from Cuba, his one-half-hour report of civilian suffering, delivered in monotone without drama even as he spoke of men, women and children dying in concentration camps by the hundreds of thousands (records studied since have confirmed the validity of his estimate) provoked outrage. People coast-to-coast took it as testimony under oath by a witness come back from Hell on Earth. Editorials, editorial cartoons and headlines flared. The "Cuban question" which had smoldered for years now ignited. Passive observation was not enough when neighbors were suffering and dying. The declaration of war in April came as the result of a passionate response by millions to Proctor's account of his ten-day tour. Proctor is the accidental father of the era of American humanitarian foreign military intervention in which we all live.

The country's passionate response may be explained further. Historical context offers us help with the paradox of such a dramatic reaction to such a non-dramatic recitation. A landslide in readiness is an apt analogy. The tense American public, hungry for information, starved for word from an intentionally mute President McKinley, who remained anxious to act well their part while the *Maine* remained a mystery, found in Proctor a lightning bolt that in an instant illuminated hundreds of thousands of suffering and dying Cubans. Their story was seized upon as the operating narrative. Suddenly, nobody needed to keep an open mind; indeed, keeping an open mind a minute longer cost lives. Proctor's narrative freed the public from the *Maine* story. The mystery of the *Maine* could rest at the bottom of the sea—Proctor vouched for a clear and attractive alternative basis for national decision-making, a story of innocent Cubans and villainous Spaniards. Rescue, over revenge, presented a nobler motive for action. And there was one last but important factor also in play: Proctor was believed when, as a battle-scarred Civil War veteran, the former Colonel of a regiment of Vermont volunteers, and a well-regarded former Secretary of War, he told the public that Spanish troops were ill-trained and poorly-supplied. Altogether, upon Proctor's statements, America's duty was obvious. In a very rare occurrence, once transcribed by reporters in the press gallery and printed in newspapers, Proctor's address was seen to be so sermon-rich with moral implications that it was literally read aloud from pulpits as a call for action. Primed by Proctor, the public awaited only some confirming word next from President

McKinley, whose "prescription" Proctor, at the end of his report, told them to expect.

But on that point, Proctor was mistaken.

McKinley was not outraged but enraged at his friend and political ally from Vermont. Although McKinley had read Proctor's notes—on the morning of March 17, 1898, Proctor had gone to the White House specifically for that purpose—McKinley had not expected any speech very soon by this characteristically silent Senator. McKinley had his own plan. McKinley, who on Christmas Eve, 1897 invited Americans to pay for peace, as it were, with massive contributions to feed starving Cubans, who personally solicited Clara Barton's promise to go to Cuba herself to run the relief effort, who secured Spain's agreement to suspend its tariffs in order to get massive shipments of food and supplies duty-free into Cuba from the United States, stood abashed. That morning in the White House, McKinley questioned the completeness of Proctor's notes and suggested that he do further research on what conditions in Cuba were ordinarily. In fact, McKinley hoped to squelch Proctor's speech. McKinley later admitted to Proctor his intention to set another Republican leader to head off his address. McKinley even questioned Proctor about timing until he understood by implication (incorrectly) that Proctor would wait a bit before he spoke. In one short speech delivered immediately, Proctor toppled McKinley's painstaking policy of patience. It did not matter to McKinley that Proctor spoke so soon after leaving him by chance, because he was hustled from the Capitol hallway to the Senate cloakroom to the Senate floor by a savvy pro-war Senator. Patronage doors wide open to Proctor closed to him during the uproar that followed his account of conditions in Cuba, an account that forced McKinley's hand.

However grudgingly, McKinley followed Proctor's lead. Before McKinley broke his silence, he knew that Americans were anxious to fight to save Cuban lives. Over three weeks after Proctor spoke, McKinley knew exactly what to say. When McKinley sent a message to Congress on April 11, 1898, he did not highlight the *Maine*. Instead, bowing to the storm Proctor had stirred up, McKinley listed four reasons to intervene in Cuba, topped by a strong country's humanitarian duty to rescue its sick and starving neighbors. Proctor's fingerprints are on that message. McKinley's echoes were not only inspired by Proctor's widely-acclaimed speech but also by a single letter—from Proctor. Riding the wave of a seemingly magical popularity, Proctor actually wrote McKinley a letter of advice in late March. Secret at the time, quoted in full in this book, Proctor's letter is preserved among the papers of the McKinley Presidential Library in Canton, Ohio. Through that letter, Proctor led McKinley to change his last line. McKinley originally intended a climactic request that Congress approve funds for Cuban relief, to Federally fund the Red Cross humanitarian project. He finally, in direct accord with Proctor's advice, omitted that plea and ended instead open to suggestion.

Thus, ironically, the War of 1898 is a war preceded by no war cries. Neither McKinley nor Proctor before him in any stirring or memorable plea asked for war. Equally ironically, Proctor's success was in a degree his downfall (albeit temporarily). Proctor risked and instantly lost his cherished role as a McKinley "insider" to save the lives of poor strangers in another country's island. Proctor's March 17 address to the Senate may be seen as an act of bravery; on that day in the Senate, Proctor stood as a profile in courage and risked his entire political future.

Subsequently events obscured Proctor's courage. An unexpectedly short war quickly followed, a relatively bloodless conflict spectacularly begun with Admiral George Dewey's one-day no-American-casualties Battle of Manila. Brief hostilities not only ousted Spain from Cuba but also left the United States an enduringly strong power with territories around the world. As McKinley and others stepped and elbowed forward for credit, Proctor had to pull strings even to be invited to the President's reception for returning veterans. But time heals all wounds. Not only did Proctor forget McKinley's slights and minimize any recalled criticism, in a sort of poetic justice, Proctor, who survived McKinley, enjoyed great terms with McKinley's successor, the zestful Theodore Roosevelt who as a Colonel of a regiment of volunteers had famously charged up San Juan Hill in Cuba. Handily re-elected, Proctor remained in the Senate until he died in 1908. However, his reputation was in large part buried with him. Because history owes Proctor more recognition than he has gotten, in this book Proctor rides again, as it were, again making his mark in history in Cuba, where he became informed and where he was inspired to draft the speech of his life, a report about Cuba, words that triggered the War of 1898.

-Wayne Soini

Chapter 1

REDFIELD PROCTOR OF VERMONT

BORN ON JUNE 1, 1831, Redfield Proctor, ultimately very wealthy, was never really poor.[2] Proctor's father, Jabez Proctor, was a well-to-do local businessman, a prosperous farm owner and an active politician. Proctor's mother, Betsey Proctor, unfortunately a much less well-documented figure, seems to have been a remarkable and frugal manager not only loved by her children but admired by them. Proctor had to deal early and often with comfortable circumstances and, although he would overcome the disadvantage of relative wealth eventually, he grew up a bit spoiled and lazy. A lack of paternal discipline, if not of parental oversight, followed Jabez Proctor's death when Proctor was eight. As the indulged youngest of four children, Proctor

[2] U.S. Congress, Redfield Proctor (Late a Senator from Vermont): Memorial Addresses. 60th Cong., 2d sess., 1908-1909, (Washington: Government Printing Office, 1909), 34. (Sen. Perkins of Calif.) Proctor's well-to-do father may nonetheless be second to the year of Proctor's birth as the cause of his later mega-rich status. See Malcolm Gladwell's provocative Outliers, The Story of Success (New York: Little, Brown and Company, 2008). At 56-63 of his book Gladwell substantiates a pattern in America's 1831-1840 male birth group. Even had he been poor, Proctor derived serious advantages from his time of arrival. Gladwell quoted sociologist C. Wright Mills, "The best time during the history of the United States for the poor boy ambitious for high business success to have been born was around the year 1835."

waxed lackadaisical. Proctor himself characterized his schoolboy years as a time when he was "more interested in roaming over the hills in pursuit of game or following streams for fish than in his books."[3] (And in that noteworthy quote work or chores do not even figure as choices.)

No previous scholar has emphasized that Proctor was raised from age 8 to 21 in a single-parent home. Proctor's mother's importance is clear but details are scarce. The familial context of Proctor's early years can only be sketched. It is nonetheless clear that Betsey, although young enough and wealthy as the widow of a "farmer, merchant, and manufacturer"[4] to be a desirable and eligible match, never remarried. This may have had something to do with the patriarchal law of those days. That is, Betsey could not consider remarrying without weighing and considering that, if she remarried, she lost to her new husband any legal right to manage her property and her late husband's estate. But Proctor never spoke of or alluded to his mother's sacrifice. Possibly, Betsey never considered single life to be a sacrifice. Perhaps Betsey thrived independently and was quite consciously content being the sole head of her household. Such key details do not survive to enable our understanding of the household dynamics.

However, if Proctor was not her favorite child earlier as her youngest, his sheer survival made him so. Betsey lost her other three adult children in a series of unrelated tragedies. Her oldest son perished far from home trying to find gold in California. Her oldest daughter, then wife of the Register of the United States Treasury, died in a steamship explosion and fire. When her last surviving daughter died of typhoid, Proctor at age 21 was Betsey's only remaining child, son and sole heir. Proctor's

---

[3] Id., 61.

[4] Ruth Lois Tweedy, "The Life of Redfield Proctor," M.A. thesis, University of Illinois (Urbana), 1942, 1.

expressed and preserved opinion of his mother that "there was no place in the world, however exalted, occupied by a woman which his mother could not have filled"[5] appears to reflect his assessment of the most gifted manager he knew, of her gender. From that comment one ventures to speculate that in Betsey a habit of practical rather than emotional concern for others may have dominated. Factually, she first became a head of household when, as oldest daughter, ten years old, her own mother died and Betsey had to grow up fast to help her farmer father raise her younger brothers and sisters, "one of whom was only a small baby."[6] One envisages a terribly young girl, then a woman, ever saddled with heavy responsibilities. Throughout marriage and into widowhood, did constantly-burdened Betsey experience a vicarious delight by freeing her son from heavy responsibilities early and into his adulthood?

Betsey, whose horizons may have been socially and geographically limited, definitely nurtured her own children to explore the world. And experiments of this kind in raising children can backfire. Freedom includes freedom to fail. Betsey presumably blessed her oldest son's decision to seek gold in California, a risky effort that cost him his life. Later, nothing, no prank, no mischief, no failure ever separated her from Proctor. She seems instead to have protected and buffered her son from any harsh consequences when he acted irresponsibly. Proctor was nearly rusticated from Dartmouth for a famously noisy prank: he set off fireworks during the speech of a visiting Congressman. How he or his mother or his uncle, the Chief Justice of the Vermont Supreme Court, or other patron managed to ameliorate penalties is obscure. What is clear is that Proctor was allowed to graduate after his stunt and his mother still presented him with substantial

---

[5] Id., 2.

[6] Tweedy, 2.

money upon his graduation in 1851. He admitted to losing it all (about $ 1,600) in Minnesota that same year under conditions that embarrassed him enough that he never later named or described his investment vehicle even in general terms. But then Proctor transformed himself. How or by what influence is utterly unclear—for want of data, one imagines Proctor listening to and learning from his entrepreneurial mother, even reclaiming lost confidence through her—but the prankster, prodigal Proctor vanished and was replaced by a new man. As a 1980 dissertation by Chester Winston Bowie[7] emphasizes, a solemn and earnest Proctor either returned home from Minnesota. Betsey did not disinherit Proctor but instead insisted that he run the family businesses. Although she had run things well enough for over ten years (and possibly for twenty if her husband's time-consuming political positions, including judge, or any chronic illness had imposed such functions on her earlier), Betsey tendered the reins of the family farm to Proctor. That Betsey had courage was immediately obvious; that she exercised good judgment was only gradually clear.

Proctor married but Betsey may also stand behind his marriage, which was to the heiress of the most prominent and wealthy family of the next town. Also, Betsey may well have encouraged, morally if not financially, his post-graduate studies at Dartmouth and then at Albany Law School. Rare in that era, Proctor went to law school *after* marrying and the birth of a son.[8] (And he went to *school* at a time that many others learned their

---

[7] Chester Winston Bowie, "Redfield Proctor—A Biography," Ph.D. dissertation, University of Wisconsin (1980). Although the M.A. thesis by Tweedy is one-quarter the size of Bowie's work, it contains some details not in Bowie, who appears not to have consulted it.

[8] Proctor's son Fletcher and grandson Mortimer both became governors of Vermont.

profession by clerking in law offices.) After her son's graduation from law school, Betsey or Proctor networked with Vermont's Chief Justice Isaac Fletcher Redfield. Redfield, the son of the man after whom Proctor had been named. Redfield stepped down as judge in 1860 after twenty-four years on Vermont's high court. Young enough, 56 years old, Redfield relocated to Boston to practice law. For no obvious reason beyond their kinship, he invited novice lawyer Proctor to join him.[9]

Their resulting partnership seems not to have been convivial. For one thing, Redfield was used to the company of learned judges and arguments by experienced advocates. In most cases, with most issues and procedures of a law office or in court, his young helper would have been a frustrating and awkward companion. For another thing, Redfield had a distinct "habit of moralizing" in his judicial opinions. The habit probably reflected his approach to life outside of court. Because Proctor in adulthood was a member of no church and more practical and political than pious, grounds for daily friction between the two men existed. Another habit probably caused yet greater friction. Redfield, Proctor's employer, was notoriously frugal. A relative visiting Boston from Vermont once asked Redfield about his worn silk hat. Redfield explained that he declined to buy a new one, preferring, he said, that "anybody who sees this one will know that the wearer of it has been a gentleman for a long time."[10] By contrast, Proctor, the natty graduate of Dartmouth and of law school, dressed well. Finally, his uncle knew the old prankster and prodigal Proctor too well ever to trust or maybe even to encourage him with any cheerfulness. Ultimately, Proctor never wrote of any fondness for

---

9 *New York Times*, April 3, 1898, magazine section, 2.

10 From "Ruminations," an article by Paul Gillies of the Vermont bar that is available on line at www.vtbar.org/Images/Journal/journalarticles/Summer%202004/ruminations/pdf (accessed 2/1/2009).

his distinguished relation; he chose war over the practice of law in Boston. As soon as war broke out in 1861 Proctor promptly fled Boston to heed President Lincoln's call for volunteers and sign on with the 3rd Vermont Volunteer Infantry.

In military service, Proctor excelled, found camaraderie and seized opportunities to lead. Popular but modest, a man concerned for his fellow Vermonters, Proctor quickly and proudly rose to major with the 5th Vermont Volunteers.[11] Disaster and even death threatened from an unexpected quarter. Proctor fell ill and, when he could deny it no longer, spitting blood, he was diagnosed with advanced tuberculosis. Mortality rates for the disease at that time was so high that this diagnosis was seen as a death sentence. Army doctors shrugged, signed a medical discharge and sent Proctor home to die. Nobody at the front expected to see Proctor again, they only anticipated hearing of his passing. Proctor's recovery was far more surprising than his infection. Once back in Vermont, doubtless with support from his wife and mother, who would have nursed him, Proctor did not resignedly take to his bed and die but instead, at first shakily and with assistance, gradually on his own, he surprised everyone by walking and, gaining distance, walked until he was strong enough to fish, then went out and fished until he was daily out walking and fishing in cool, dry mountain air. Proctor's cure was neither sudden nor certain, a relapse was always possible. Incredibly, though, within six months, somewhat fleshed out, well enough to fill out his uniform slenderly,[12] Proctor imposed upon his doctor to deem him fit. Instead of dying Proctor was back in the service where, being an experienced veteran, he was unanimously elected colonel of the 15th Vermont Volunteers.[13]

---

11 *New York Times*, April 3, 1898, magazine section, 2.

12 On the basis of unknown source(s), Tweedy said that Proctor "returned to action in the fall, although his cough remained." Tweedy, 7.

13 *New York Times*, April 3, 1898, magazine section, 2.

Proctor, then and thereafter almost mystical in the belief that he literally owed his life to Vermont, was fully prepared to stand with other Vermonters in battle to the death.

Bearing arms in early July, 1863, he was at first assigned with his 15th to the center of Cemetery Ridge at Gettysburg, precisely where Pickett's Charge would come close to overwhelming its Union defenders during fierce and bloody fighting. Waved away as if by some protecting angel, Proctor's regiment was reposted at the last minute with auxiliary troops. Even so, Proctor endured campaign hardships and saw action at Centreville, Fairfax Court-House and on other battlefields.[14]

But none of the battles Proctor fought shaped his personal future so dramatically as a single promise that he made and lived to keep. Proctor, certainly not going back to Boston or ever practicing law with a relative again, either thought of something else or simply leaped upon the option as attractive. At some point during the war, Proctor and Wheelock Veazey, a lifelong friend and the colonel of the 16th Regiment of Proctor's brigade,[15] promised to become law partners should they both survive. When they both survived, they did open a small law office together in Rutland. Their office unexpectedly became Proctor's springboard into business and, thereby, to unimaginable wealth as Vermont's "marble baron." Indeed, Proctor soon left their somewhat prosperous law firm entirely to Veazey shortly after the Sutherland Falls Marble Company fell into financial difficulty. That was because Proctor, assigned to the quasi-judicial

---

14 Tweedy, 7.

15 G.G. Benedict, Vermont in the Civil War, A History, (Burlington, Vermont: The Free Press Association, 1888), Vol. 2, 411.

role of receiver for that small, failing marble mill,[16] saw in the mill a rare opportunity rather than a chore usually undertaken by lawyers as a routine series of bill collections, dunning letters and lawsuits. After going over the books in his humble and marginal role, Proctor wooed a larger, more stable marble firm to merge with Sutherland Falls.

Of this still-small operation Proctor, the receiver, all but a fly on the wall, still on the fringe, gambled on the boom-or-bust, volatile marble business, by boldly buying shares for himself. He sought to own and control the new operation. Having bought at his price such shares as he could in Vermont, he copied names and addresses from the company list of shareholders and went beyond Vermont to find them. That quest, by horse and train, took him all around New England. Among others, he went to John Spaulding, an investment banker in Boston who owned a good block of stock in the Sutherland Falls Marble Company. Proctor planned to purchase Spaulding's shares but his obvious enthusiasm became an obstacle. Proctor's blossoming business acumen came through to Spaulding in their one-on-one conversation. After their interview, Spaulding declined to sell. "I like your spirit and your plan and I would like to stay in with you," Spaulding told him. He made a different offer, telling Proctor, in an experienced broker's vote of confidence that confirmed Proctor's judgment and further whetted his desire to take the plunge, "You can have my proxy to vote as you wish and if you need any more money I will put in my share."[17]

---

[16] The *New York Times*, April 3, 1898, magazine section, 2, said that Proctor was named receiver "by choice of all parties" to a litigation involving the Sutherland Falls company. No source was given.

[17] Frank C. Partridge, "Redfield Proctor, His Life and Public Services." *Proceedings of the Vermont Historical Society for the Years 1913-1914* (1915), 69.

Spaulding's turnabout turned out to be typical. Proctor, one on one, could not make a bad impression on businessmen. Not only stockholders but competitors wanted Proctor as company followed company in merging with Proctor's small original two-mill operation. Ultimately, thyere were but two big firms in Vermont marble. One was Proctor's and the other was the Rutland Marble Company. As he set his sights on his major competitor, the Rutland Marble Company offered Proctor the position of manager.[18] Proctor actually managed the two companies until he could consolidate them both as the Vermont Marble Company and become its president.[19] The originally local company of two to three hundred workers had, in Proctor's hands, grown into a multi-quarry, multi-million-dollar enterprise with over 1,500 workers.[20] Proctor's management had been good. His organizing abilities, delegation of duties, close oversight of budgets, cost-cutting measures founded a business monopoly out of a previously loosely-run group of competitors. Beginning 1893, Proctor's new but cash-rich company[21] was solid and solvent enough to weather the worst depression the country had ever known.

All through this time, Proctor had never ceased to act as an organizer and frequent generous underwriter of veterans' reunions in Vermont. That same activity spawned and maintained a network of loyal war veterans, the core of the all-male electorate, who enabled Proctor, a poor public speaker, to stand successfully for office. Veterans voted Proctor into a seat in the Vermont legislature, then made him the state's lieutenant governor and, finally, its governor.

---

[18] Id., 70.

[19] Id.

[20] *New York Times*, April 3, 1898, magazine section, 2.

[21] Proctor's company never made less than $ 100,000 in annual profits during the 1890's.

Besides veterans' reunions, banquets and excursions, Proctor funded a tuberculosis sanitarium. He also established libraries, clinics and paid to build churches for his workers in the town named in his honor, Proctor. When nobody else would establish a bank needed in a growing community, he did the legwork and sent funds in the new bank's direction. He was practical and civic-minded but he could also be grandly sentimental. Proctor never forgot his old war horse, a Morgan stallion he permitted to graze on his lawn. When "Old Charley" died, Proctor had his body buried on his landscaped estate by Otter Creek. In a further remarkable tribute "Old Charley's" grave, an especially "well-kept plot,"[22] was solidly and permanently marked by a twenty-ton block of choice Vermont marble.[23]

[22] *The Vermonter*, Vol. 9, 350 (July 1904).

[23] Clipping, n.d., Proctor Archives, Proctor Free Public Library, Proctor, Vermont, (hereafter, "PFPL"), Folder 7, Box 19.

Chapter 2

REDFIELD PROCTOR, NATIONAL FIGURE

HAVING RUN UP THE LADDER of state offices, Proctor handed off the reins of his established and global enterprise to his son, Fletcher, and joined President Benjamin Harrison's cabinet as his Secretary of War. In that office Proctor performed predictably well. A bundle of energy, the former colonel and savvy businessman brought the Army to attention and up to a degree of efficiency and greater accountability than in years. Among other projects, Proctor revised the code of military justice, merged pension divisions into a single bureau, established promotional examinations, initiated annual written personnel evaluations and regular, signed, dated inspection forms of all Army posts. Proctor basically reduced the possibility of concealing deficiencies and, when his system exposed bad conditions and inept commanders, he took quick and decisive action. His combination of exposing deficiencies and taking action paid dividends in morale. In fact, the Army's desertion rate dropped by half.

In a drama that played itself out mostly in the South, Proctor got the most press, and regional notoriety, during a unique controversy that arose when Jefferson Davis died. No law required the lowering of flags to half-mast upon the death of a former Secretary of War but such was the custom. When Jefferson Davis, who had once served as Secretary of War but who was far better known for having been the President of the Confederate States of America, died Proctor declined to lower the national flag in his honor. Southern editors took offense, their newspapers were critical, and there were even some public outbursts.[24]

However, the incident probably did him no harm in Vermont, where Proctor remained alert for his next step up the political ladder. When a senate vacancy suddenly arose in Vermont, by resignation of a "Silver Republican," George Edmunds, Proctor had good cards to play. In wooing Governor Carroll Page, who could be counted upon to appoint a fellow Republican to fill out Edmunds' unexpired term, Proctor's particular cabinet position provided him with unusual clout and Proctor capitalized on it in fine style. Proctor invited Page, a former large-scale dealer in rawhide, for a grand tour of the Army posts of the West.

One imagines that Proctor, who excelled at enthusiastic one-on-one conversations, sold the Governor on appointing him during their train ride West. Or he may have said nothing and let great generosity be reciprocated naturally. Either way, directly or indirectly, Proctor had plenty of time to demonstrate that his contacts in Vermont remained strong, to remind Page that his business interests were a literal cornerstone of the Vermont economy, and to display that his political acumen was never sharper, dropping names to illustrate his record of placing Vermonters into good Federal jobs and in sponsoring public projects in Vermont. Any such unrecorded words aside, the exotic settings and the excitement of cavalry maneuvers, flag-waving and bands greeting and welcoming committees toasting to the health of the honored guests would have favorably impressed and pleased

[24] Bowie, 260-262. Bowie said that some Mississippians hanged Proctor in effigy, wearing a placard, "Redfield Proctor, Coward." No reaction by Proctor is documented. Indeed, he seems not to have ever engaged the flag issue publicly.

Vermont's chief executive, who may have even found a little time to reminisce with his old contacts in the rawhide business that made his fortune. Upon his return from the West, Governor Page named Redfield Proctor to be the state's interim senator. Proctor's election and re-election followed his interim appointment.

Proctor, who never listed the reasons he wanted to become a senator, certainly did not go into the senate for an audience. Despite Proctor's success as a businessman one-on-one with another businessman, when a certain calm and deliberative tone was persuasive, similarly-crafted public addresses fell flat. "He never strove after effect in oratory,"[25] George L. Rice told the knowing Rutland audience at Proctor's memorial service. Roger Cooley, who wrote a dissertation of Proctor's Vermont years, viewed Proctor as a man who "loved a good time and was naturally gregarious . . . always a mixer among men whom he knew in political, military or professional circles"[26] but mute before more than a handful of people. Indeed, Proctor's correspondence rather than speeches provided Cooley with almost all of his Proctor quotes. Even at reunions of Civil War veterans, an activity which Proctor enjoyed immensely, did not motivate him to speak at any length or fluently. Cooley wrote that

> the bent some men had for oratory was not Proctor's. Indeed, one has but to examine the occasions of his later life, in the sessions of the Legislature or Congress to note that he seldom spoke, and then usually from a written text. Yet his presence was always felt [at veterans' reunions] and he was always called upon to contribute some word to the occasion. When he did,

[25] The clipping from this unidentified newspaper was hand stamped March 16, 1908, PFPL.

[26] Cooley, 384.

> it is possible to detect an uneasiness in the remarks that were recorded.[27]

Speaking posthumously and politely about a public person who could not speak, Representative Haskins gave it his best spin. He said that Proctor's "speeches were prepared with great care and delivered without the least semblance of passion, but in the most quiet manner and without any attempt at display."[28] Haskins opined that it was "not his purpose to stir men's blood, but to appeal to their reason and better judgment."[29]

Coloring muteness, "imperturble calm" was said to characterize Proctor in office.[30] Vermont's junior senator, in public silence, a public figure of *gravitas*, scribbled notes and made deals via quiet chats, primarily securing Federal patronage for fellow Vermonters. Dutifully performing the subterranean and invisible homework, a close reader of official reports whose opinion was especially valued by less literate colleagues, Proctor also rose by dint of seniority to chair the Committee on Agriculture and Forestry beginning 1896.[31] He made few headlines but Proctor, a businessman who loved nature at the very time that farming was becoming a business, was popular enough with farmers, whom he favored for Federal subsidies.

None of this suggests a clue about any Cuban connection except that Proctor was known, when known at all, to be a reliable and reticent but savvy Senator.

---

[27] Id., 169-170.

[28] Memorial, 72

[29] Id.

[30] *The Vermonter*, Vol. 13, 71, (July 1908).

[31] Partridge, 89

Chapter 3

SENATOR PROCTOR, McKINLEY'S FRIEND

By dint of Proctor's efforts, including marches of Civil War veterans wearing gold ties in support of the Gold Standard, popular vote for McKinley exceeded that of all other states. (Eighty per cent of Vermont's electorate voted for McKinley.) Proctor could have had a cabinet post; he much preferred ready access to McKinley. The Green Mountain landslide entitled Proctor to his own reviewing stand of McKinley's inaugural parade. On March 4, 1897, Proctor presided over the Vermont McKinley Club at the corner of Pennsylvania Avenue and 12th Street.[32] The inaugural committee, which included fellow Vermonter Colonel Myron M. Parker, who would later

[32] According to Bowie, Vermont was the only "state" to have its own reviewing stand. Bowie, 337. Technically, the "Vermont" stand was the "Vermont McKinley Club's" private stand. "During the campaign Proctor led a procession to McKinley's front porch. Republicans wearing lapel pins for McKinley and gold-colored neckties sang to their candidate, 'We want yer, McKinley, Yes, We Do." Leech, 92. Proctor had also been one of a handful of McKinley's economic advisors.

go with Proctor to Cuba,[33] relaxed rules to permit the stand to be constructed. He further made certain that the Vermont National Guard, taking part in an inaugural parade for the first time, marched near the beginning of some 20,000 "soldiery and civilians."[34] Led by Governor Grout on horseback, the Vermonters were fifth among all states represented.[35] If ebullient Governor Grout approached the Vermonters' reviewing stand as he did the President's, he dashed up on his white steed, and reined in his horse to stand as he doffed his hat and threw back his cape with a flourish.[36]

Despite the display of uniforms, the campaign of 1896 had actually been waged on monetary policy. Proctor and his invitees gathered behind a huge banner which proclaimed, "Vermont Gave McKinley 80% of Vote, No Other State Gave Him over 69%. Sound Money and Protection."[37] McKinley, who spoke often about gold, made no speeches about Cuba. He only briefly considered addressing the Cuban question in his inaugural speech. That is, he reached out to his Secretary of State-designate, John

---

33 *The Vermonter*, Vol. 2, 138 (March 1897). The "executive committee in charge of the inauguration" included Vermont-born Colonel Myron M. Parker (a District of Columbia builder and realtor who had served on the same committee for Presidents Garfield, Harrison and Cleveland). Proctor wrote of Parker that he had been "a good soldier" in the 1st Vermont cavalry in Custer's brigade and worked after the war in the post office in the District of Columbia before becoming a "man of business" who was prompt, competent and personally popular. Parker may also have once shared Proctor's affliction of tuberculosis, as Proctor mentioned a "severe and protracted illness" which Parker overcame. Proctor letter to William McKinley recommending Parker as marshall of the District of Columbia, January 30, 1897, PFPL, Folder 36, 225.

34 *New York Times*, March 5, 1897, 1.

35 Id., 2. Only the President's home state, Ohio, the Vice President's home state, New Jersey, New York and Maryland preceded Vermont.

36 Id.

37 Photograph, *The Vermonter*, Vol. 2, 129 (March 1897).

Sherman, for suggestions. But when Sherman sent him "a rather inconsistently worded memorandum, stating that intervention was, in Sherman's belief, inevitable . . . McKinley mulled over this advice, editing it and cutting out the conclusion. In the end he discarded the whole memorandum."[38]

The inaugural audience, including outgoing President Cleveland, heard nothing about Cuba. McKinley instead affirmed generally the policy of non-intervention and paid a gracious compliment to Cleveland on his peaceful settlement of the crisis over Venezuela.[39] Perhaps baffled by McKinley's utter silence about Cuba, Cleveland was moved to warn his successor. During their ride back together to the White House, Cleveland reluctantly cautioned McKinley, "I am deeply sorry, Mr. President, to pass on

---

[38] H. Wayne Morgan, William McKinley and His America, (New York: Syracuse University Press, 1963), 102.

[39] McKinley spoke generally and approvingly of "the policy of non-interference with affairs of foreign governments wisely inaugurated by Washington," while being "ever watchful of our national honor, and always insisting upon the enforcement of the lawful rights of American citizens everywhere." More specifically, McKinley declared, "We want no wars of conquest; we must avoid the temptation of territorial aggression. War should never be entered upon until every agency of peace has failed; peace is preferable to war in almost every contingency. Arbitration is the true method of settlement of international as well as local or individual differences." In this respect, he singled out the treaty of arbitration between the United States and Great Britain to resolve the Venezuelan boundary dispute, then pending Senate ratification, as a "glorious example of reason and peace, not passion and war, controlling the relations between two of the greatest nations in the world, an example certain to be followed by others . . ." McKinley urged early action by the Senate as "a duty owed to mankind." Moreover, he said that the "moral influence of the ratification of such a treaty can hardly be overestimated in the cause of advancing civilization . . . I cannot but consider it fortunate that it was reserved to the United States to have the leadership in so grand a work." McKinley's inaugural address is available at http://avalon.law.yale.edy/subject-menus/inaug.asp (accessed 1/11/2009).

to you a war with Spain. It will come within two years. Nothing can stop it."[40]

Whether McKinley believed Cleveland or not, he quickly decided to send someone to Cuba.[41] Offner called this decision the first step McKinley took toward creating a Cuban policy.[42] He asked one of his closest friends and near neighbor,[43] Judge William Rufus Day, to go. Proctor knew all about it and wrote to Paul Brooks in Rutland that Judge Day "goes ostensibly to inquire into Dr. Ruiz' death yet his real mission will be doubtless to give the President his view of the situation."[44]

But soon after Proctor wrote that letter, McKinley realized that he needed Judge Day in Washington. The titular Secretary of State, John Sherman, whose memorandum on Cuba McKinley had rejected, was feeble if not senile,[45] and McKinley wanted Day to help with foreign policy. (Indeed, when war came, Sherman

---

[40] H.H. Kohlsaat, From McKinley to Harding, Personal Recollections of Our Presidents, (New York: Charles Scribner's Sons, 1923), 64.

[41] Proctor's proximity to McKinley's Cuban plans is illustrated by a letter he wrote to Brooks while Day was still intended as the Administration's man in Cuba. "I hope Judge Day's visit there may be productive of good . . . though he goes ostensibly to inquire into Dr. Ruiz's death yet his real mission will be doubtless to give the President his views of the situation. I tell you in confidence that Mr. Partridge would have joined with him on the mission except for the condition of his health, for which as you know he is now in the Adirondacks." The reference to the Adirondacks implies tuberculosis. Redfield Proctor to Paul Brooks, April 10, 1897, PFPL, Folder 7, 349.

[42] Offner, 42.

[43] Duncan, 37. "The Day home in Canton was only three doors away from that of the McKinleys." Duncan said that, after the 1896 election, when too many guests showed up for McKinley to see, Day would take them in at his house.

[44] PFPL, Folder 7, 348-349. Dr. Ruiz was an American citizen whose death in a Havana jail was considered suicide by the Spanish but murder by American reporters. The matter remains mysterious.

[45] Morgan, 255-256.

resigned and Day became Secretary of State in title as well as function.) In April McKinley named Day Assistant Secretary of State[46] and hastily recruited another friend,[47] William J. Calhoun, who "knew nothing of Cuba and the Spanish language"[48] but who had served with the Major in Congress, to go to Havana.

McKinley's first choice to be his minister to Spain, John W. Foster, former Secretary of State and former American minister to Spain, declined. He joined Cleveland in telling McKinley that he was sure of war between the United States and Spain.[49] That virus seemed wide-spread as McKinley's next six candidates refused. McKinley must have been relieved when a one-term Congressman and former lieutenant governor of New York recommended by "Boss" Platt,[50] Stewart L. Woodford,[51] said yes. A complete lack of diplomatic experience[52] may account for Woodford's willingness to debut in foreign affairs as the American minister to Spain in 1897. The good news was that Woodford had an intense interest in Cuba. The bad news was that he was a member of the "Cuban League" of New York.[53] In short, Woodford sympathized with the

---

46 Joseph Eregina McLean, William Rufus Day, Supreme Court Justice from Ohio (Baltimore, The Johns Hopkins Press, 1946), 30, cited the *New York Daily Tribune*, April 24, 1898. ("The nomination . . . came as a surprise not only to the public but to Day himself.")

47 Kevin Phillips, William McKinley (New York: Henry Holt and Company, 2003), 93, called Calhoun "one of (McKinley's) political operatives." However, Calhoun's place in the official family may have been more peripheral. Dawes had to prod McKinley to appoint Calhoun as Interstate Trade Commissioner. Charles G. Dawes, A Journal of the McKinley Years, (Chicago: The Lakeside Press, 1950), 137, 142.

48 Offner, 42.

49 Offner, 55.

50 Offner, 55.

51 Id.

52 Id.

53 Id.

insurgents. Nonetheless, having found a person willing to be his minister to Spain, McKinley appointed Woodford his minister to Spain.

McKinley let Cleveland's consul, Fitzhugh Lee, stay on in Havana. Given the refusals he met in filling the post of minister to Spain, he may have decided not to cast about for anyone new in Cuba. Or McKinley may have positively felt that in retaining Lee, he kept one experienced hand in the game. In any case, the downside of the renewed Lee appointment was that McKinley insured that his regular reports from Havana would be biased. As John Tone noted,

> (o)ne of the Cubans' most important allies was U.S. consul Fitzhugh Lee. The nephew of Robert E. Lee, a former Confederate cavalry commander, and the ex-governor of Virginia, Fitzhugh Lee was an indispensable political asset. This made his ignorance of Spain, Cuba, and the Spanish language forgivable and even useful . . . (d)espising everything about Spain and Spanish culture . . . [54]

The first emissary sent out, William Calhoun, returned from Cuba with disturbing news. Reporting inconclusively on Dr. Ruiz, Calhoun told the President on June 22, 1897 of an island "wrapped in the stillness of death,"[55] of war by terrorism, war by attrition. From whatever sources[56] Calhoun got it right. Cuba was in ruins. The guerilla insurgents and the Spanish army

---

[54] John Lawrence Tone, War and Genocide in Cuba, 1895-1898 (Chapel Hill: The University of North Carolina Press, 2006), 222-223.

[55] Lewis L. Gould, The Presidency of William McKinley (Lawrence, Kansas: University Press of Kansas, 1980), 67.

[56] Tone, 210. ("Calhoun's sources are not clear . . .")

were locked in a bloody and deadly impasse. As Lewis Gould summarized in data-rich 1980:

> To win the war the Cubans followed a strategy that made the most of their limited military resources. Avoiding battles with the numerically superior Spanish, they directed their energy against the Cuban economy. By destroying crops, disrupting transportation, and engaging in incessant hit-and-run assaults, the rebels pinned down Spanish soldiers and ate away at the island's economy.[57]

McKinley decided to ignore the Cuban insurgents. It was a significant determination. All of McKinley's communications were directed to Spain. After Calhoun's report, McKinley warned the Spanish minister, Don Enrique Dupuy de Lôma, that the war in Cuba must be "conducted according to the military codes of civilization."[58] McKinley sent nothing to the insurgents, although they had engaged in terrorist tactics themselves. McKinley basically echoed Calhoun's report[59] and said to de Lôma that Spain must not use "fire and famine to accomplish by uncertain indirection what the military arm seems powerless to directly accomplish."[60]

Through this drama, Proctor, on the sidelines, an observer at best, remained an unlikely speaker and unlikely champion of the Cuban cause. Before 1898, nothing in his record suggested radicalism, or foreign affairs interests or any charitable inclinations

---

[57] Gould, 60.

[58] Id., 67. The warning was given on June 26, 1897.

[59] Morgan, 25. (Full quote: "I traveled by rail from Havana to Matanzas. The country outside of the military posts was practically depopulated. Every house had been burned, banana trees cut down, cane fields swept with fire, and everything in the shape of food destroyed.")

[60] Gould, 67.

outside of the United States proper. Proctor's evolution into an effective advocate for the dying *reconcentrados* of Cuba in 1898 faced no fewer than five obstacles. First, Proctor, with no demonstrated expertise in foreign affairs, spoke no foreign language. He crossed the border only to hunt and fish at four sportsmen's clubs he belonged to in Canada. Second, Proctor personally discounted Cuba's distress. Before he went to Cuba himself, Proctor judged news accounts of Cuban suffering to be exaggerated and unreliable. Third, after three years of civil war, Cuba in 1898 was a police state in ruins, Havana itself a hazardous place for a genteel 66-year-old millionaire to visit, let alone the rest of the island. Fourth, a Congressionally-sponsored fact-finding tour of Cuba of 1898 was in place for which others had been selected. Fifth, and perhaps most important, Proctor rarely spoke in public. A politician always in the wings and never center-stage, Proctor's forte was private and confidential, off-the-record conversation.

But these obstacles were all being worked on, undermined and subverted, ink drop by ink drop, in letters dictated in Rutland, Vermont. Paul Brooks, an obscure but wealthy man with an unknown illness. Cuban-born, a Vermont transplant who may have suffered a paralyzing stroke or some other crippling affliction that led him to Vermont and mountain air as a cure, composed letters in his sickbed. His daughter, Pauline, took her father's dictated letters to Proctor regularly. Receiving them—information Brooks received from Cuba and passed on as reliable facts, as a holocaust was occurring just off the American shore—Proctor mulled over going to Cuba to see for himself. Proctor had visited Havana once before to check on a potential marble quarry in Cuba. Brooks urged him to go again, to inform himself, to see for himself. More than any one person or event letters from Paul Brooks stimulated Proctor to see Cuba again that winter.

Chapter 4

McKINLEY'S PEACE PLAN AND THE RED CROSS

That summer McKinley was critical of Spain. Spain's answer was received coolly. On August 26, 1897 the frustrated Spanish foreign minister asked Woodford, McKinley's brand-new minister in Madrid, to tell McKinley that Spain was doing no more than the Union army had done during the American Civil War.[61] On September 18, 1897, former Union Army Major McKinley, doubtless with clenched teeth and through tight lips, authorized Woodford to ask "whether the time has not arrived when Spain . . . will put a stop to this destructive war"[62] and said ominously that the United States wanted a reply by November 1.[63]

After the assassination of hard liner Antonio Cánovas del Castillo, a new government under Pràxedes Mateo Sagasta and his liberal party inherited that November 1 deadline. On October 9, 1897, at its first meeting,[64] Sagasta's new cabinet took a symbolically potent first step. They decided to recall General Valeriano Weyler Nicolau,[65] the general known in the American

---

[61] Id., 68.

[62] Id., 69.

[63] Id., 68.

[64] Charles S. Olcott, The Life of William McKinley (Boston: Houghton Mifflin, 1916), 396.

[65] Gould, 68.

press as "Butcher" Weyler. After Weyler's recall, in early November, Sagasta officially suspended Weyler's reconcentration policy itself and declared an amnesty for political prisoners.[66] On November 25, Sagasta officially proclaimed autonomous Cuban home rule, effective January 1, 1898. He reserved only control of the military and foreign relations for Madrid.[67]

Madrid's momentum encouraged McKinley finally to address the Cuban question publicly.[68] Cleveland had said much about Cuba in his final state of the union message.[69] In his first state of the union message, McKinley determined to do so, too. He seems likely to have consulted with Day. Shippee and Way, biographers of Day, even concluded that Day co-drafted the long Cuban section

---

[66] Gould, 69.

[67] Id.

[68] Morgan, 47. "This seemed the logical time to break his long silence." For most Americans, December 6, 1897 would be recognized as the date of McKinley's first statement about Cuba. Morgan himself noted, without considering it to break McKinley's silence, a June 26, 1897 dispatch that Secretary of State Sherman had sent Spain, "the first official statement of (McKinley's) Cuban policy," Id., 27, a protest "in the name of the American people and in the name of common humanity" that "a war, conducted almost within sight of our shores and grievously affecting American citizens and their interests . . . shall at least be conducted according to the military codes of civilization." Id, 27-28.

[69] On December 7, 1896, with ninety days left in office, Cleveland said in his final annual message to Congress, "It cannot be reasonably assumed that the hitherto expectant attitude of the United States will be indefinitely maintained. While we are anxious to accord all due respect to the sovereignty of Spain, we cannot view the pending conflict in all its features, and properly apprehend our inevitably close relations to it, and its possible results, without considering that by the course of events we may be drawn into such an unusual and unprecedented condition, as will fix a limit to our patient waiting for Spain to end the contest, either alone or in her own way, or with our friendly cooperation." Gould, 65. McKinley, thus, complemented Cleveland's message with "mission accomplished—maybe."

of McKinley's message.[70] With Cuban autonomy announced and about to go into effect, McKinley, perhaps in Day's words, told Congress that "(t)he near future will demonstrate whether the indispensable condition of a righteous peace, just alike to the Cubans and to Spain as well as equitable to all our interests so intimately involved in the welfare of Cuba, is likely to be obtained." As a stiffener to Madrid's resolve he added, "If not, the exigency of further and other action by the United States will remain to be taken."[71]

But McKinley and Day were already taking action. Although he said nothing about it to Congress, McKinley had recruited Clara Barton to end the suffering of hundreds of thousands of Cuban peasants which McKinley saw as the chief source of friction between Spain and the United States. Displaced from their land, herded on short notice with few possessions into so-called *trochas*, guarded night and day, but not cared for, the peasant *reconcentrados* sickened and died without clean water, sufficient food, basic sanitation, minimal clothes or decent shelter. McKinley felt that saving the *reconcentrados* was the key to peace. McKinley and Day arrived at an audacious, unprecedented, ingenious and participatory plan to save them. If McKinley failed, he would fail in full public view, for what McKinley and Day imagined was rescuing the *reconcentrados* through the voluntary charity of the American people.

The president of the American Red Cross, pivotal to any such peace plan, was headquartered a block away from the White House and near the War Department, State Department and the Capitol. Clara Barton, a legend since the Civil War, often visited

---

[70] Shippee and Way, "William Rufus Day," The American Secretaries of State, 59, quoted in McLean, 39. They said that it bore "the marks of Judge Day's collaboration and those of the President."

[71] Gould, 70.

all of the above.[72] McKinley's brainstorming session with Day on Cuba was just ending when Barton dropped by the White House on November 30, 1897. McKinley invited her into their council.

Cuba was not only on the President's agenda. By November 30 Cuba had been simmering in Red Cross planning sessions without action for months. Barton displayed no reluctance in front of McKinley on November 30 but for about a year she had been wary of Cuba. Her wariness had historical cause. Overseas relief was an old and fundamental question for the American Red Cross. For its first ten years, it sponsored disaster relief projects in the United States only.[73] Its overseas work began almost by accident during the Russian famine of 1891. A Red Cross-friendly newspaper editor in Iowa importuned Barton to help move surplus corn to where it was needed.[74] Not deigning to refuse, publicity-conscious Barton raised funds for a ship, arranged for railroads to carry the corn at no cost, got famine-related telegrams dispatched free, made steamship agents waive commissions, and

[72] Miss Barton's service during the Civil War included two years as a member of General Benjamin Butler's staff. Barton wrote that Alger "had two Senators with him. We waited. Finally, he sent word to come, only one Senator was there. I declined and would leave but when the messenger remarked that the guest was Senator Proctor, I went at once(,) had a most cordial interview with Sen. P. who related to Sec. Alger his recollections of the interview with General Butler on me in his office . . ." Barton Diary, Library of Congress, microfilm, (November 30, 1897).

[73] Although William E. Barton, The Life of Clara Barton, The Founder of the American Red Cross, (New York: AMS Press, 1969), 2 vols., 217, lists "Balkan War" 1883 among domestic disasters for which American Red Cross was given, that reference is not detailed, although the other matters are, 219-31. Moreover, Balkan War assistance may have involved implementation of obligations under the Treaty of Geneva, which the United States signed in 1882. The Russian Famine relief was undertaken by Barton's decision.

[74] A good, succinct summary of this first American Red Cross overseas relief project appears in David H. Burton, Clara Barton, In the Service of Humanity, (Westport, Connecticut: Greenwood Press, 1995), 122-123.

cajoled insurers to charge no premiums. Filled with over 200 trainloads of Iowa corn, enough to feed 700,000 people for a month, the ship Barton chartered left New York harbor under a Red Cross flag.[75] Everything she did for the Russians was done in the United States. Other organizations did more. But publicity about this Red Cross overseas project led the National Armenian Relief Committee[76] to Barton as an expert in 1895. They asked her to help the "starving Armenians"[77] of Turkey. She agreed and, this time, she followed the food overseas.

Once in Turkey, she quickly faced two unanticipated obstacles. First, the Turkish foreign minister required the diplomatic fiction that Clara Barton the individual, not the American Red Cross, was in Turkey with "her" supplies.[78] After Barton accepted this condition, the National Armenian Relief Committee, unsympathetic with the unauthorized deal, almost broke with her.[79] "Barton's" work in Turkey, credited solely to her, was accomplished to a steady drumbeat of criticism and nitpicking from New York. At one point Barton ludicrously wrote to the Committee, "We will finish the job without further aid."[80] She nonetheless pressed on, did effective work under trying conditions, and saved lives. Ultimately, the Turkish government awarded her a medal,[81] the American press hailed her as a hero, and Barton was life-long wary of overseas projects.

---

75 Id., 123.

76 Peter Balakian, The Burning Tigris, The Armenian Genocide and America's Response, (New York: HarperCollins Publishers, 2003), 68-70.

77 Id., 75. The Turks were engaged in genocide in Turkish Armenia. Balakian believes that Barton originated the "starving Armenians" phrase, much used thereafter in characterizing the target of relief efforts.

78 Id., 78-79.

79 Burton, 129; Pryor, 292.

80 Burton, 130.

81 Id.

Cuba was the first test of her resistance to another overseas relief project. Newspapers began to howl for the Red Cross to help the Cubans even before McKinley swore into office.[82] Of course, Barton needed not reply and did not. But by the end of McKinley's first hundred days, Barton was sensitive to building pressure. She confided to her diary on June 13, "I feel by the trend of things that the breeze is blowing a little too brisk in the direction of relief for Cuba to be quite secure for us."[83]

Exactly the next day during the "Lend a Hand Club of Ladies" of Baltimore trip with Miss Barton up the Potomac to Mount Vernon, Red Cross board member Jannet Richards "made a Cuban speech on the boat and revealed the plan of the leading ladies of Washington to call friends for the Red Cross to distribute in Cuba and ask us to go."[84] Barton described herself in her diary as the minister who was afraid that they would not raise the money, and still more afraid that they would.[85]

The ladies acted in concert at the next Red Cross board meeting. Mrs. Thurston, the wife of Nebraska Senator Thurston,[86] officially moved to raise $ 10,000 by selling ten-thousand one-

---

[82] *New York Tribune*, January 10, 1897, used the precedent of Armenia in its editorial for Cuban relief by the American Red Cross. Pryor, 296.

[83] Barton Diary, LC, Reel 4, Containers 5-6 (June 13, 1897). Barton wrote of herself alternately in the first person, the third person (as "CB"), and by the imperial "we" or "us."

[84] Id., (June 14, 1897).

[85] Id.. ("I am like Henry Ward Beecher at sea—'I am afraid they won't raise it, and still more afraid they will.") See also Burton 1995, 131. According to him, Barton tagged the Cuban relief enthusiasts, who were all wives of men in or formerly in high governmental positions, "the court ladies."

[86] Senator and Mrs. Thurston took part in a visit to Cuba sponsored by the *New York Journal*. The Thurstons, Senators Gallinger and Money, and Congressmen Cummings and Smith arrived in Havana on the same day that Proctor left. Barton, 546. Mrs. Thurston, described by Barton as "worn, frail" died during that visit. Id., 516.

dollar donation receipts for an *ad hoc* Washington-based "National Relief Fund for Cuba in aid of the American Red Cross."[87] The speech-maker from the boat, Mrs. Richards, present at the meeting, may have been the wind behind the sails. In her diary, Barton dutifully sketched the donation receipt design into her diary while she lingered mournfully over the motion that failed to pass, the motion to keep the Red Cross out of Cuban relief.[88]

Barton was resistant to consider Cuban relief before the American public was ready and she continued to gauge the public unready. She wrote on July 4, 1897 that she did not think that public sentiment favored "any real humanitarian relief"[89] to Cuba.

Women who disagreed brought the board's dispute to the White House. By clandestine appointment, Mrs. Ellen Forster and a Mrs. Kilvert[90] saw the President about Cuba. Barton was furious to learn that they had "taken the lead, stolen a march on us" and met with McKinley and Day. Worse, Barton heard that they had "gotten assurance that they have no doubt but when the time comes, and the money is raised, and conditions favorable but the way will be entirely clear, so far as the Government is concerned. Secretary Day advised them to address a letter directly to Mr. de Lôma."[91]

Barton herself rushed to the White House, where she had the satisfaction of hearing McKinley ask her about the ladies, "What do they <u>intend</u> to do? What did they <u>want</u> to do? How did they

---

87 Barton Diary, LC, (June 22, 1897).

88 <u>Id</u>.

89 <u>Id</u>., (July 4, 1897). ("It does not appear to us that under the present state of feeling and public sentiment that any real humanitarian relief can be given in Cuba.")

90 <u>Id</u>., (July 12, 1897).

91 <u>Id</u>.. In this passage Miss Barton seems to parody a strong of nice-sounding bland assurances to which inexperienced ladies attached greater meaning than she did.

expect to accomplish it?"[92] McKinley recounted that Day had suggested that any letter to de Lôma be written by Barton. The ladies had demurred, insisting that Barton would not write one. Only then had Day suggested that they write their own. Barton scribbled waspishly into her diary that McKinley told her that "something should be done to prevent them from doing real mischief in the excess of zeal and scarcity of knowledge."[93]

Cuba did not go away. Barton simply waited the "court ladies" out. On Thanksgiving she heard from a confidante that she had "no more to fear from the Ladies' Cuban Relief Committee,"[94] Barton decided that the time had come to act. On Saturday, November 27, she went alone to the Spanish consulate. The de Lômas were away but Barton learned that they were expected back on Monday.

On Sunday, November 28, 1897, she wrote, "I am still thinking of Cuba as an open door. We will go to see Mr. de Lôma tomorrow in search of what may develop."[95]

She saw the Spanish minister on November 29, and proposed that a few Red Cross officers enter Cuba to "distribute, unmolested, among its starving *reconcentrado* population such relief as the people of America desired to send."[96] Minister de Lôma gratefully suggested that Barton write a note that he would add to his weekly diplomatic pouch to Havana on Wednesday.[97]

On the morning of November 30 Barton quickly wrote an inspired three-page letter. Revising "not one word," she brought it personally to the White House. There McKinley, in conference

---

[92] Id., (July 12, 1897).

[93] Id.

[94] Barton diary, LC, (November 25, 1898). (The exact sentences was, "They have learned their ground better.")

[95] Id., (November 28, 1897).

[96] Barton, 515.

[97] Barton Diary, LC, (November 29, 1897).

with Day, explained their plan to her, and asked for her help. For her part, she showed her letter. She proudly told her diary that night how McKinley declared, "That is a good letter."[98]

Other letters had reached McKinley before Barton's draft. These were secret letters from the five American consuls in Cuba that reported raging typhus epidemics, unburied dead, starving women, children, and elderly, people in rags or naked.[99] Nothing was exaggerated, although statistics are debated to this day. John Tone summarized this somewhat macabre scholarly debate concerning the Cuban holocaust:

> We will never know the exact number of Cuban civilians who died under reconcentration . . . (E) conomic historian Jordi Maluquer de Motes has suggested that between 155,000 and 170,000 Cubans died due to reconcentration. This is the most careful calculation performed to date using the census data. But this figure was too high for other scholars. David Trask and Joseph Smith thought the number of fatalities should be placed closer to 100,000.[100]

In November, 1897 a figure of 300,000 fatalities, or one-tenth of Cuba's civilian population,[101] seemed credible—and, even more frighteningly, things were getting worse. As John Tone wrote, "One of the terrible ironies of reconcentration is that the worst mortality occurred after Weyler's departure . . . on October 9, (1897)."[102]

---

[98] Id.

[99] Tone, 198-200.

[100] Id., 209-215.

[101] The figure 300,000 was used by Calhoun and Lee in 1897. Proctor adopted it, apparently satisfied that it was accurate, if not conservative, in light of the scale of suffering he had observed.

[102] Tone, 217.

McKinley, then more aware than anyone in America about deadly and worsening conditions in Cuba, asked Barton how soon she could leave for the island. Her estimate of two or three weeks disturbed him.

"Oh, you must not defer a day," he told her. "The suffering is terrible. You must take the first conveyance after your reply from Cuba."[103] It was probably that day that McKinley confided to Barton his specific intention to make "a personal appeal to the people of the United States" to relieve "the perishing people of Cuba."[104] With her letter approved, Barton hastened back to de Lôma. With almost naïve delight, she proudly recorded in her diary that de Lôma pronounced her letter "simply perfect."[105] The sun set on November 30 at the end of a perfect day for Barton.

The Spanish minister sent Barton's letter the next day. Madrid obviously read it as a terrific letter as well. In early December, the Queen Regent granted permission for an American Red Cross relief mission to open in Cuba.[106] McKinley worked in parallel to clear a remaining obstacle out of the way. Cuban customs duties comprised a wall to relief that Spain must pull down. The day after Barton's visit, on December 1, 1897, McKinley sent Minister de Lôma a list of goods which he proposed be exempt from duties if donated by Americans to suffering Cubans.[107]

---

[103] Barton diary, LC, (November 30, 1897).

[104] Clara Barton, "Our Work and Observations in Cuba," 166 *North American Review* 552 (May 1898) (Reprinted and bound, New York: AMS Press, 1968). Barton specified no date of her first awareness from McKinley of his personal intention. Although November 30 seems right, Barton's diary entry for November 30 does not include this shared confidence.

[105] Id.

[106] It is likely that permissions arrived after December 6, the date of McKinley's state of the union message.

[107] *Boston Globe*, (December 25, 1897), 4.

In response, Spain waived duties on all of the goods McKinley proposed and more.[108]

With tariffs down and Barton in line to go to Cuba, McKinley and Day set tottering Secretary of State Sherman in motion. Stating that he acted at the express direction of the President, Sherman issued a press release on December 24, 1897. It said that Consul General Lee in Havana was ready to receive contributions of money and donations of specified food, clothing and medicines, all duty-free. Sherman's invitation concluded:

> The President is confident that the people of the United States, who have on many occasions in the past responded most generously to the cry for bread from the people stricken by famine or sore calamity, and who have beheld no less generous action on the part of foreign countries when their own countrymen have suffered from fire and flood, will heed the appeal for aid that comes from the destitute at our own threshold and, especially at this season of good will and rejoicing, give of their abundance to this humane end.[109]

The President's confidence was misplaced. Barton, America's most experienced veteran of relief logistics, exhibited little patience with a plan that everybody send everything to our man in Havana. In her diary on December 25, 1897, (her birthday), Barton wrote without further comment, "Notice in morning paper of a call from the Secretary of State for aid from the American people

---

[108] Id.

[109] *Boston Globe*, (December 25, 1897), 4. The reference to "famine" evoked the 1891 famine in Russia, in which the American Red Cross sent a shipload of grain, and "flood" evoked German Red Cross assistance on site after the 1889 Johnstown Flood.

for Cuba."[110] The next day, although without specifics, Barton decisively noted in her diary that she would write Judge Day and the President concerning Sherman's appeal.[111]

Judged by immediate result, Barton was right. Then as now, Secretary of State Sherman's Christmas Eve appeal was one of the least memorable events of 1897. And yet, whether it was practical or not, his notice was one of enormous significance in American history. Through Sherman, McKinley took a giant step on December 24, 1897. Although it remains obscure, on that date an American President, without Congressional sanction, made a public commitment to the relief of foreign citizens in a foreign land. Swaddled in condonation by the Spanish government, Secretary Sherman's December 24 notice was camouflaged as an announcement by two governments acting in concert. But the old man's short press release sounded reveille on American foreign policy limited to the interests of American citizens. On that day and in that way the State Department made the American government's interest in suffering foreign civilians official.

As a fund drive, newspapers reported success, headlining that Day cabled $ 5,000 to Consul Lee on December 28, 1897.[112] It was true in fact but not representative of reality. The $ 5,000 was from one donor, President McKinley himself, anonymously at the time.[113] The historic hybrid of a government-sponsored relief

---

[110] Barton diary, LC, (December 25, 1897).

[111] Id., (December 26, 1898). In her memoirs Barton seems to have airbrushed and conflated events. She said nothing about Sherman's appeal. Instead, she described her own organization's 1897 failure to raise funds. With some humor, she depicted a supposed *Red Cross* press release stating that it was ready to receive contributions, after which it received "not one dollar." Such an effort is nowhere corroborated by her diary. In fact, Sherman's press notice is the only one mentioned in her 1897 diary.

[112] *Boston Globe*, (December 29, 1897), 6.

[113] Morgan, 150.

project funded privately drew but a single breath before Clara Barton intervened.

Barton got the fund drive out of Washington. Barton had professional reasons to know that New York City and Boston contributors together accounted for about half of the Armenian relief money. It was logical that a Cuban relief committee be established and headquartered either in New York City or in Boston. New York was the more obvious choice because it hosted an active Cuban League, insurgent "junta" members, and Cuba-mad Hearst and Pulitzer newspapers. On January 1, 1898, after talking to the Second Assistant Secretary of State Alvey Adee, [114] Barton triggered a new Central Cuban Relief Committee by naming her nephew, Stephen E. Barton,[115] chairman of a three-man board in New York. Within two weeks, the committee began its distribution of a series of graphic press releases concerning sick, starving and dying Cuban civilians, primarily women, children and the elderly.

Taking over fund-raising from McKinley's inexperienced hands, Barton's second-wind Cuban relief campaign was a spectacular success. By way of comparison, it had taken an entire year for the Armenian relief committee to raise the sum of $ 116,000.[116] Barton's Cuban relief committee raised almost twice that, over $ 200,000, within its first two months of operation.[117]

---

[114] Barton Diary, LC, (January 1, 1898). Barton said that she "talked over Cuban Matters" with Adee on January 1, then described setting up the committee and planning to leave for Cuba personally "by the next steamer." Adee may have had a creative role in these plans, or Barton may have simply wanted to give the State Department notice of a "competitor" fund raising body, whether Adee agreed or not.

[115] Barton, 275, identified Stephen E. Barton as Clara Barton's nephew and as a person who took part in many different Red Cross activities.

[116] Burton, 130.

[117] *For. Rel.*(1898), 753.

Barton made obsolete her own comment in July, 1897, that she did not think that public sentiment favored "any real humanitarian relief"[118] to Cuba. Prodded by her committee in New York, a new national constituency grew and flourished in which it was respectable, even conventional, to care about Cuban civilians. Best of all, so smooth was the transition that no one noticed the regime change from McKinley to Barton. Even so, the McKinley-Barton relief mission widely understood to be the last, best hope of peace. Those who tracked diplomacy noted that Spain and the United States had found common ground and jointly cooperated. Americans who only saw humanity in need gave readily, invested in the Red Cross emotionally, and hoped to save the fragile peace by peacefully saving the *reconcentrados.*

[118] Id., (July 4, 1897). ("It does not appear to us that under the present state of feeling and public sentiment that any real humanitarian relief can be given in Cuba.")

Chapter 5

McKINLEY SPEAKS SOFTLY

As 1897 ended, McKinley not only sent Congress his state of the union message and organized his Red Cross relief plan, he also drew a line firmly around Sagasta's reforms. Woodford was directed to tell Sagasta that he had entered upon "a pathway from which no backward step is possible."[119] The Cuban reforms McKinley welcomed were not universally popular even in Cuba. Episodes of civil disorders called "riots" by many but actually rowdy protests, street theater, took place in Havana in late December, 1897, and mid-January, 1898. Noisy crowds milled for hours around autonomy-supporting newspapers. Slogans were shouted but nobody was hurt and no government installations were ever circled or seized. Spanish soldiers did not stifle these events but took part in them. Ultra-Spanish partisans hoped to provoke Madrid to reinstate Weyler.

Weyler never returned to Cuba. An American warship did. When Day asked if an American ship might make a "courtesy call," Minister de Lôma said that such visits should never have been interrupted. Both men hoped that the resumption of visits by the American Navy to Havana would symbolize the return of better days. There was no disorder when the *Maine* put down anchor in Havana harbor on the morning of January 25. The first American warship to visit Havana since revolution

[119] Gould, 73.

broke out in the spring of 1895[120] became a floating symbol of *rapprochement.*

Two days later, on the evening of January 27, McKinley hosted the annual dinner for Washington's diplomatic corps. The three ambassadors of England, France, Germany and the minister of Spain sat at his table. McKinley spoke cheerily to Minister de Loma, saying, "I see that we have only good news." What he was referring to was majority Congressional support for his policies. "You, who comprehend this," McKinley went on proudly to de Lôma, "will understand how strong our position is and how much it has changed and bettered in the past year; you have no occasion to be other than satisfied and confident."[121] McKinley, having also launched the Cuban relief effort which was enjoying accelerating success in raising money and contributions in kind, believed that he would preserve peace between Spain and the United States.

What remained was to work out an armistice. If McKinley could conjure a respite in the fighting, then arbitration or mediation could achieve a civilized resolution of the struggle. In a word, he could achieve in Cuba what Cleveland had achieved in Venezuela. Of the men at the head table the most aware of the Venezuelan precedent would have been the British ambassador,

---

[120] *Chicago Tribune*, March 18, 1898, 2. Day reminded reporters on the evening of March 17, 1898, that the *Maine* was the first American warship to visit Havana since early 1895.

[121] Gould, 72.

to whom Cleveland's. Secretary of State Olney had written[122] bombastically on July 20, 1895, that, "To-day the United States is practically sovereign on this continent, and its fiat is law upon the subjects to which it confines its interposition . . . its infinite resources combined with its isolated position render it master of the situation and practically invulnerable as against any or all other powers."[123] Diplomacy after Olney's letter averted hostilities, continuing talk led to a treaty signed on November 12, 1896.[124] It was the treaty McKinley urged the Senate to approve when he swore into office. An international commission was arbitrating the Venezuelan dispute in Europe as McKinley, speaking softly, sought to nudge Spain toward armistice and arbitration as well.

In fact, relations between Spain and the United States were deteriorating as diplomats ate and drank. McKinley spoke too softly to be heard. The gap between McKinley's optimism and the average American's displeasure with Spain may never have been greater. Nothing, not even public silence, works forever to maintain peace. And McKinley spoke with de Lôma not having re-entered into dialogue with the American public. McKinley's biographer H. Wayne Morgan judged that McKinley's "reticence

[122] http://www.unc.edu/depts/diplomat/archives roll/2001 10-12/bridges adee/bridges adee p . . . at p. 1 (accessed 6/9/08). "The note was Olney's, but the drafting was largely done by (Alvey Augustus) Adee." "American Diplomacy; A Look Back; An Appreciation of Alvey Adee," an article by Frank Cass, at Plainly a neurotic, Adee spent time closely scrutinizing the annual Colonial Office List of Great Britain. He found 33,000 more square miles noted for British Guiana in 1886 over the 1885 edition. When Adee brought this datum to the attention of his superiors, they brought it to the attention of the President. Cleveland considered it not a boundary dispute but a sneaky violation of the Monroe Doctrine.

[123] Robert E. Welch, Jr., The Presidencies of Grover Cleveland (Lawrence, Kansas: University Press of Kansas, 1988), 183.

[124] Id., 186.

was always his flaw as a leader,"[125] but his criticism is overbroad. Precisely by keeping his mouth shut McKinley kept his options open and avoided war with Spain for over a year.

Public silence about Cuba bought time until Sagasta became Prime Minister. But Sagasta's quick recall of General Weyler, amnesty and proclamation of an autonomous government in Cuba beginning January 1, 1898, required a public response. Accordingly, McKinley had material for a "State of the Union" message to Congress that featured Cuba prominently. McKinley kept to himself his November 30 plea to Clara Barton and his urgent December 1 request that Spain lift some Cuban tariffs. The tone of McKinley's message to Congress was one of cautious optimism.

McKinley wanted to follow Cleveland's route to peace with Britain over Venezuela. He foresaw arbitration rather than war. Nonetheless, he could not arbitrate with Spain over any Cuban issues while *reconcentrados* were starving and dying. His consuls were telling McKinley that there were dead unburied in the streets near the consulates. Less than three weeks after his message to Congress, he issued a Christmas Eve press release through Secretary of State Sherman that better reflected the precariousness of peace and the necessity for action. Food for peace was his plan.

But life is full of acts and unintended consequences. Beginning January 1, 1898, when McKinley's Christmas Eve charity morphed into the Central Cuban Relief Committee, the cultivation of public opinion moved outside of McKinley's control. Not only did McKinley's silence fail to stifle concern, McKinley's silence amplified the words of others. His half-blessed Cuban Central Relief Committee distributed propaganda pieces, bulletins of Cuban distress. In their wake, a cacophony of reports appeared in the press trumpeting massive shipments of food, clothing and

[125] Morgan, 69.

medicines for *reconcentrados.* Absent narration by McKinley, the bulletins and shipments on a scale well beyond those sent to the starving Armenians destroyed any sense of progress in American minds. Morgan's criticism of McKinley's public silence, invalid throughout 1897, achieved merit. Beginning January 1, 1898, intensifying concern over Cuba without a word from McKinley preceded February 15, 1898, when the *Maine* exploded in Havana harbor. Even then, McKinley resumed silence, excusing himself as he waited for a report from the naval board on the cause of that explosion. By March 17, 1897 McKinley provided the background silence which allowed the deep bass voice of Redfield Proctor, by great irony one of McKinley's closest allies, to stand in the Senate chamber and rouse the country into indignation with his short eyewitness report. But to give the report, Proctor had to see Cuba first.

Chapter 6

SENATOR PROCTOR'S CUBAN TRIP

THE OUTDOORS REMAINED HIS AVOCATION, especially fishing and hunting. His friend Frank Partridge said, "It was this love of nature which all his life made his greatest recreation hunting and fishing."[126] A fellow Senator was sure that Proctor's "greatest pleasure and recreation were found in the use of the gun and the rod."[127] Proctor was acknowledged by Native American guides as a great woodsman. One said that "he could move through the woods more silently than any white man"[128] he ever saw. Proctor hunted wild boar,[129] and frequented Canada for salmon in season.[130] Also, in the winter Proctor sometimes went south to fish. It turned out to be important to American history that he long planned to get to Miami in February, 1898 with his old fishing buddy, Colonel Myron M. Parker.

---

[126] Id., 67. Partridge said that Proctor "never caught fish nor shot game beyond what could be used for food" and that "he would never fish nor hunt on the Sabbath." Id.

[127] Memorial, 35.

[128] *The Vermonter*, Vol. 13, 32, (March 1908).

[129] Photograph captioned, "Redfield Proctor, Corbin's Park," n.d. Box 19, PFPL

[130] Photograph captioned, "Tobique Salmon Club, New Brunswick, Canada," n.d., Box 19, PFPL.

Proctor's unexpected added side trip to Cuba began in Vermont. From Rutland, a city some five miles from Proctor, Paul Brooks wrote his senator. An invalid too ill to sit up and write, possibly the victim of a stroke, Brooks dictated letters to his daughter. He asked Proctor to pay attention to Cuba. Brooks was an American citizen born in Cuba about 1838 who after some education in the United States became a sugar exporter[131] in eastern Cuba. He married a woman from Vermont and, apparently upon suffering his disabling illness in his late fifties, he retired to Rutland to recuperate. It was from his sick-bed that Brooks maintained a steady fire of words in behalf of Cuba Libré and, very gradually, wore down Proctor's resistance to seeing Cuba.

Brooks contacted Proctor no later than 1895, when still-hale Brooks served as the American consul at Guantanamo during the Cleveland administration. Brooks was led by geography to observe close-up the insurgent side of the civil war because the eastern side of Cuba was early taken and permanently held by rebels. Brooks prematurely signaled the imminent fall of Spain. When Cleveland's Secretary of State, Olney, passed the word up, Cleveland issued a series of stern admonitions to Madrid.

Defending his silence a year before his speech, Proctor excused himself from speaking about Cuba. He wrote Brooks

[131] As documented through ancestry.com, the 1850 census indicates that one Paul Brooks was attending a boarding school in Chester, Pennsylvania at age 12. In its shipping records, one Paul Brooks is noted as having left Santiago, Cuba, for the United States as a "merchant" in 1891, and as a "planter" in 1895, each time with his wife (Sarah, about seven years younger than he) and daughter, Pauline, born about 1862. Assuming that Sarah was not Paul's second wife and Pauline's step-mother, then Pauline was born when Sarah was about 18 and Paul was about 25. Younger children were also traveling with them in the 1890's. If Percy, born about 1888, and Anita, born about 1892, were also his children and not Brooks relations, then Sarah continued to bear children up to about age 37, when Paul was about 44.

in April, 1897 that "it is always bad policy in a legislative body to talk any more than absolutely necessary, and by too frequent repetition we become accustomed and hardened to the story of wrongs and outrages there."[132] But, as he admitted in his speech of March 17, 1898, Proctor was not convinced of the veracity of stories of wrongs and outrages. Proctor did selectively share some of Brooks' messages with hand-picked Republican leaders,[133] but, until February, 1898, he made no move to visit Cuba.

Brooks wrote to politicians other than Proctor. After all, Secretary of State Olney took Brooks' reports from Cuba for President Cleveland to read personally. And Brooks certainly kept contact with Cuban insurgents. Among letters he gave Proctor were introductions to rebels on the island, letters which Proctor never used.

But no matter how many people Brooks wrote, Proctor was an odd choice. Did Brooks simply write to both of his Senators? Did Proctor and Brooks meet in Vermont? Were there family connections?[134] Or was Brooks drawn to Proctor's reputation for compassion as one who founded a tuberculosis sanitarium, a hospital, churches and libraries in Vermont? In any case, as a shrewd man, Brooks was doubtless aware that in each letter he was asking a settled Republican *doyen* to become a maverick, a

[132] PFPL, Folder 7, 348 (April 10, 1897).

[133] Id., 349.

[134] Proctor wrote Senator Frye about Brooks in 1895, recommending him as a source of information about Cuba. Frye was enormously interested in Cuba. Proctor likely hoped to pass the torch of Cuba to one more willing to carry it. To Frye Proctor described Brooks as a well-informed Cuban consul who was spending "the summer and fall in Rutland near here," who "married his wife there, a Miss Sheldon," and by that marriage became an American citizen. Brooks' father, an Englishman, had settled in Cuba "early in this century and was very successful in business." Redfield Proctor to William P. Frye, August 23, 1895. PFPL.

domestic politician to engage in foreign affairs, a conservative to become a liberal. Facing near-certain failure, Proctor's ailing pen pal displayed incredible persistence.

There is evidence, by way of an unintentionally amusing reply to Brooks, that Proctor encouraged him to look for succor elsewhere. On December 18, 1895, Proctor hinted to Brooks to approach others as follows:

> Am glad to hear from you. Hoped I might have another talk with you before I left Rutland, but was absent much of the time for the last two weeks. Did you meet any other Members of Congress? You spoke of going to Senator Frye, but I think you did not do so. The sympathy for Cuba is very general,—I might say universal . . . [135]

In the end Brooks was only partly successful. Of three aims Brooks achieved one, that Proctor visit Cuba. To achieve even that, Brooks prodded Proctor without positive feedback for at least a year. Brooks also wanted Proctor to speak with his Cuban insurgent friends, something Proctor never did, and, lastly, Brooks failed to recruit Proctor's support for the insurgent cause.

The Cuban trip long urged upon Proctor as a duty[136] was not on Proctor's schedule until after the *Maine* blew up in Havana harbor. Proctor planned to go only to Florida during winter of 1897-98 with his fishing buddy, Colonel Parker. Parker was a Vermonter who resettled in the District of Columbia after the Civil War. Starting as a humble postal worker, Parker had become

---

[135] Redfield Proctor to Paul Brooks, December 12, 1895, PFPL.

[136] Id. ("I greatly regret that I had not gone to Cuba a year ago at least and seen for myself . . .")

a prominent and prosperous property developer.[137] Touring Cuba was a chore Proctor did not relish and a hardship, presumably, he did not want to impose on his friend. Brooks sent Proctor letters of introduction to his Cuban informants, but Proctor himself only made tentative, cursory preparations. From Secretary of War Alger he reserved a possible military escort, Army Lieutenant H.R. Lemly,[138] but he warned Lemly on February 6 that his "plans in regard to Cuba are very indefinite,"[139] and, on February 15, "exceedingly doubtful."[140] Also on February 15 Proctor wrote his son Fletcher, "I may go to Cuba, but doubt it very much."[141] That night the *Maine* exploded. Suddenly defensive of his heretofore-indefinite plans, Proctor wrote Fletcher on February 17, "I shall go to Cuba if I feel like it and we do not have war before I go."[142] Finally, just before boarding the night train for Florida on February 18, Proctor wrote to Fletcher without further explanation but with an underlined emphasis about going to "Florida and probably Cuba."[143]

---

[137] Bowie, 361. Myron C. Parker, was "a friend and wealthy Washington real estate owner." Proctor wrote a recommendation of him as a Vermonter who had served with the 1st Vermont Cavalry in Custer's Brigade. Following a "severe and protracted illness" (tuberculosis?), Proctor said that Parker had regained robust health and was prompt, competent and popular. Proctor to McKinley, January 30, 1897. Box 8, Folder 36, 225, PFPL.

[138] These facts are deduced, i.e., Lemly could not self-assign and Alger was a friend of Proctor's. The author found no primary document which directly substantiates either this deduction or the deduction that Lemly ultimately did escort Proctor in Cuba. Neither Proctor during his speech nor anyone's account of the trip refers to Lieutenant Lemly.

[139] Bowie, 357.

[140] Id.

[141] Id.

[142] Bowie, 359.

[143] Id.

His Florida trip proved to be no day at the beach. Proctor and Parker were shadowed everywhere by reporters. Senator Proctor, the President's known confidant and a former Secretary of War planning to see Cuba, was a reporter's dream come true. They speculated that Proctor was studying how long it would take to mobilize troops in Miami and how to transport them.[144] His trip to Cuba was headlined as planned in order that the American consul in Havana could receive information "too important to be entrusted to wires even in cipher."[145] Proctor's fishing trip in Florida was taken to be an amusing "cover story." Even after Proctor was on the island, where he did no fishing, the *New Haven Leader* wrote waggishly:

> He has been very busy fishing all the time. Indeed, so devoted is he to the sport, that he has fished on land, in the sea and all over the island. (He) ought to have some mighty interesting fish stories to relate. Perhaps President McKinley will listen to some of them.[146]

Before he set off for Cuba Proctor told a reporter, "To tell the truth, we are going over there to see what's going on, to be where the excitement is. Doesn't everybody want to go there? Don't you? There isn't a bit of political significance about it."[147]

But this was not in essence true. Boyish curiosity did not motivate the 66-year-old Senator to see what the excitement was. Proctor had laid the groundwork for real fact-finding. He took Brooks' letters of introduction letters with him, although he did not use them. He explained to Brooks later that "after seeing

[144] Id., 360, citing the *Cincinnati Inquirer*, n.d.
[145] Id., 361, citing the *New York Journal,* n.d.
[146] Id., 362-363.
[147] Id., 361, quoting *Boston Advertiser,* February 26, 1898.

the conditions I wished to hurry home, and to have gone among the insurgents would not have strengthened my views at all."[148] Apparently not to offend Brooks, he did not mention that he had other letters of introduction he did use, addressed to Cuban businessmen.

Senator Proctor said in 1898 and for the ten remaining years of his life that his visit to Cuba was unofficial. "I wish you would deny positively that I am here on official business,"[149] Proctor asked American reporters when he was interviewed on arrival in Havana. Senator Dillingham nonetheless suggested a governmental motive behind Proctor's trip in his memorial address on Proctor in 1908:

> The debates preceding the declaration of war against Spain showed such lack of authoritative information of existing conditions in Cuba and, as a consequence, such wide differences of opinion among Senators as to the policy which ought to be adopted by the Government that he was filled with apprehension, and with characteristic forethought and following a lifelong practice to seek the fullest knowledge of underlying conditions upon which to base his

[148] Proctor to Brooks, March 29, 1898, Box 8, Folder 38, 456, PFPL.

[149] *New York Daily Tribune,* February 27, 1898, quoted in thesis by Ruth Lois Tweedy, "The Life of Redfield Proctor," University of Illinois (Urbana), 1942, 39. (Full quotation: "I have no mission. If I had any official duty I would not have been a week getting here. I am not in any sense a representative from President McKinley nor do I have anything to do with the Court of Inquiry (on the *Maine*). I shall call on Captain-General Blanco and the naval officers here as a private citizen. This trip is no new idea. Mr. Parker and I take two or three trips every year, hunting and fishing . . . I wish you would deny positively that I am here on official business.")

> judgment and action, he, on his own responsibility, at his own expense, sought by a personal visit to Cuba to ascertain the real conditions there existing.[150]

It was true that facts were important to Proctor. As Secretary of War Proctor had both identified and rectified a data logjam in the Army. He initiated a regular stream of specific written reports from Army posts to Washington. In order to foster

> promotion upon the basis of merit he instituted what are now known as the "Efficiency Records." He provided that special studies pursued, special work done, the reports of superior officers and all other material bearing upon the record and professional proficiency of each officer should be preserved . . . to furnish a record by which officers might be impartially judged and wisely employed.[151]

The establishment of that "information technology system" was his lasting accomplishment. It was arguably ingrained in Proctor to detect and to correct factual impediments to informed decision-making. But Dillingham aside, it is utterly unclear that Proctor intended to gather information to cast informed votes as a Senator on war or peace, or to advise McKinley or Day, or even to share with the public. Furthermore, his calculus of motivation may likely have changed toward sharing data publicly because of what he learned, how confident he was of his mastery of the facts, and how urgent the situation was for some of his fellow human beings.

During his speech Proctor later exposed that his original focus had been the economic impact of the Cuban civil war. "I

---

[150] Memorial, 18.

[151] Partridge, 81.

had letters of introduction from business friends at the North to bankers and other businessmen at Habana," Proctor said, "and they in turn gave me letters to their correspondents in other cities. These letters to businessmen were very useful as one of the principal purposes of my visit was to ascertain the views of practical men of affairs upon the situation."[152]

Americans headed for Cuba in the late 1890's were advised that Havana offered some sanctuary from its civil war. Billy Bitzer, a burly, beer-loving 25-year-old, a hand-cranker, one of the world's first newsreel cameramen, arrived in Havana with his camera on February 19, 1898. "Visiting Cuba under Spanish rule was highly dangerous," he later wrote. "I had been warned beforehand to go straight to the Ingleterra Hotel, where I would find comfort and safety."[153] Outside Havana, Cuba lay in ruins.[154] But Havana he described as "orderly," a city in which one could travel "alone, without hindrance." Even Captain Sigsbee of the *Maine* recalled feeling comfortable in Havana before his ship exploded.[155]

In Havana Proctor had ready access to Cuban and American government officials and could make contact with English-speaking businessmen to whom he had letters of introduction. He

---

[152] Id.

[153] G.W. Bitzer, Billy Bitzer, His Story (New York: Farrar, Straus and Giroux, 1973), 34. Bitzer stayed until the day Consul Lee evacuated in April. He made the only movies of the hulk of the *Maine* in Havana harbor.

[154] José M. Hernandez, "Cuba in 1898," at http://www.loc.gov/rr/hispanic/1898/hernandez.html, accessed 11/19/08. "The conflict, combined with the Spanish-U.S. tariff controversy of the 1890s, had destroyed two-thirds of its productive capacity. Close to 20 percent of its prewar estimated population of 1,800,000 had perished, and for those who survived the future was bleak indeed. Cubans had no capital and were heavily in debt." Hernandez estimated "the poverty-stricken masses" at 500,000 "inarticulate, largely illiterate and apathetic" Cubans.

[155] Charles D. Sigsbee, The "Maine," An Account of her Destruction in Havana Harbor, (New York: The Century Co., 1898), 47.

doubtless began to hear about the *reconcentrados*. "It was impossible to be in Havana without hearing much about *reconcentrados*," Sigsbee wrote in his memoirs. Sigsbee found the Spanish civilians "perfectly frank and outspoken in their admissions of the terrible suffering and death that had been wrought."[156] Proctor, who likely would have been content with Havana hearsay, had barely arrived before he and Parker ran into Clara Barton.

Barton had kept her promise to McKinley. She had arrived with J.K. Elwell of Ohio, on February 9,[157] their boat steaming past the stars and stripes of the *Maine* at its anchorage. Elwell, who spoke Spanish and had run a shipping concern in Santiago for six years,[158] was in Havana to oversee the peace project. He volunteered in response to Consul Lee's request to the Committee for a private citizen to organize the unloading, storing and distribution in Cuba of the American-donated food, supplies and medicines. Barton dined aboard the battleship at a gala reception held on the evening before the ship went down. When the explosion rocked the city twenty-four hours later, Barton headed to help survivors, arranged for funeral processions and burials of the dead in a hillside cemetery in Havana and telegraphed updates to Washington.

Proctor and Parker met her some ten exhausting days later, when Barton was planning to leave Havana. She thought that

---

[156] Id. Sigsbee theorized that openness flourished about the plight of the *reconcentrados* because each side, Spanish and Cuban, blamed the other for the *reconcentrados*' misery.

[157] This is the statement in her memoirs. In her May, 1898 magazine article Barton stated that *she* had been requested by Consul Lee "to follow (the supplies) to Cuba and assist in the distribution." Barton, 553. The Southern-born nephew of Robert E. Lee was not likely to have requested that a lady enter a war zone. Barton's memoir formulation is preferred. Barton went to Cuba with Elwell, rather than the reverse.

[158] Barton, 519.

she saw kindred spirits. In what may have been a projection on her part, she characterized Proctor and Parker as wanting to see conditions of the island's population "to gain some practical knowledge which could be used for their benefit."[159] Further confident of the old soldiers' abilities to scout out such practical knowledge, Barton said that there

> seemed to be no more certain way of their gaining this information than by inviting them to accompany us on the various tours of investigation which we would be now able to make outside of Havana. Reports of great suffering had come in from Matanzas, and it was decided *that* should be our next point of inspection . . . Our own small party was joined by our Washington friends . . . [160]

With Parker, in Barton's group, Proctor traveled by carriage, ferry-boat and rail, almost every day. He ultimately toured four of the six provinces of Cuba. The Barton group's first stop was Matanzas.[161] In Matanzas, Proctor's first sight of *reconcentrados* had to be his most shocking. In Havana the Red Cross had opened four stations for distribution of bread, at which some 12,000 ragged needy stood in line for rations.[162] But in Matanzas there were no rations at all. Nothing had yet arrived from Havana. Proctor saw the most pitiful sights. As one previously greeted by beggars in Havana, he was struck by how rarely in Matanzas he was

---

[159] Barton, 531.

[160] Id.

[161] Barton, 554.

[162] Id. On December 14, 1897, Consul Lee in Havana estimated 150,000 destitute civilians were then in and near Havana, of whom he estimated half would die, given inadequate food provided by Spain. *Chicago Tribune*, April 12, 1898, 9.

approached by any *reconentrado*. He saw men, women and children paralyzed into apathy. "Rarely is a hand held out to you for alms when going among their huts," he later told the Senate. These were huts he described as being "about 10 by 15 feet in size, and for want of space usually crowded together very closely. They have no floor but the ground, no furniture, and, after a year's wear, but little clothing except such stray substitutes as they can extemporize."[163] As to sanitation, he said that "conditions are unmentionable."[164]

On rail lines to and from such sights Proctor studied the passing countryside, noting destruction and assessing the state of the Spanish military. His long-time friend and political aide, Frank Partridge, verified not only that Proctor "was fond of things military" but also that he "had a quick perception of technical military question."[165] Unlike members of the official delegation that stuck close to Havana, all without military expertise, Proctor sized up Spanish readiness for war as he toured with the Red Cross.

Although he never spoke of any anxiety, he traveled through contested territory during a civil war, exposed himself to contagious diseases and lived uncomplainingly for trips where rudimentarily decent conditions did not exist. By a strategy that insured that his investigation could not be faulted as either biased or incomplete, Proctor kept his eyes open, asked questions in English as he got around Havana and the contested areas, and pointedly declined to meet with rebel spokesmen or even to correspond with them.

But a bias was surely forming. In a letter written from Washington only a month after war was declared, Proctor wrote Brooks that he intended to devote himself almost entirely to "Cuba and her welfare."[166] This specific vow probably reflected a

---

163 *Cong. Rec.*, 55th Cong., 2nd sess., 1898, 2917.

164 Id.

165 Partridge, 79.

166 Proctor to Brooks, May 25, 1898, Box 8, Folder 39, 175, PFPL.

resolution formed in Cuba itself. Proctor returned to the United States transformed. His formerly ostentatious indifference about going or not going to Cuba, of going if he felt like going, was gone. He said little. He ducked reporters' questions. One exception is hardly an exception. When an innovative New York reporter cornered him as captive interviewee on the train to Washington, Proctor evaded with pomposity, opining broadly that settlement of the Cuban question "must come from outside the island. It depends upon the future action in Spain and in the United States."[167]

But he wrote. He penned seventeen pages about Cuba by the morning of Thursday, March 17, 1898, when he went to the State Department. He wanted to obtain and incorporate suggested revisions before he had the manuscript typed and copied for distribution as a press release. Of course, Proctor bypassed aged and infirm Secretary Sherman for the "true" Secretary of State, Day, who had given Proctor the letter of introduction to the American Consul.

Day reviewed Proctor's factual commentary and found nothing exceptionable.

But before leaving Day, Proctor, for some never-explained reason, asked him if it would be better to hand his data out to reporters or to recite it in the Senate. Likewise for no stated reason then or later Day answered, "The Senate."

With that from Day, Proctor went to the White House to McKinley. Proctor's recollection of their conversation ten years later, after McKinley had died, when Proctor himself was nearing his own end, was no misty reminiscence of a warm exchange.

The only statement Proctor reported after McKinley went over his notes was negative. McKinley said, "You have not said

---

[167] *New York Daily Tribune*, March 11, 1898, quoted in thesis by Ruth Lois Tweedy, "The Life of Redfield Proctor," University of Illinois (Urbana), 1942, 41.

that the normal condition of the Cubans is entirely unlike the normal condition of the Americans."[168] McKinley, although publicly mute, thus insisted upon his proprietary mastery of the complexity of Cuba. His snappish critique scorned Proctor's notes as a schoolboy essay lacking in historical perspective. Desiring no argument, Proctor instantly agreed to amend his report.

McKinley intended that Proctor proceed with caution on his incomplete draft. McKinley insisted that Proctor expand his statement and when Proctor seemed to approve his suggestion McKinley thought that they were agreed that the manuscript was not final.

McKinley's suggestion had been a poison pill. McKinley hoped that Proctor would strangle his speech rather than deliver it. After all, for Proctor, no expert, to make a comparison of Cuban and American conditions before 1898 in suitable detail and accuracy for presentation to the United States Senate and to the nation on the public record would take time. And simultaneously, Proctor's first-person account would slide toward becoming balky congressional rhetoric of the very type Proctor dreaded.

Proctor certainly told McKinley about his conversation with Day. McKinley did not directly challenge Day's advice. He instead slyly asked Proctor if he intended to present his statement to the Senate that day.

"I don't think I shall," he told the President. "It is simply a draft in pencil and I had thought of having it typewritten."[169]

McKinley spoke twice with the same aim, to buy time. He needed time because the Navy's report on the *Maine* was nearly complete and could be in Washington within a week. Silence by everybody in the interim would keep all options open. Proctor, notes in hand for a speech, initially rattled McKinley but Proctor's

---

[168] Linderman, 55.

[169] Id.

answer that he did not expect to speak to the Senate that day defused tension—and soon proved to be an unfortunate *gaffe*. Proctor's long-standing closeness and rapport with the President was nearly at an end.

Chapter 7

SENATOR PROCTOR'S "SPEECH"

SENATOR PROCTOR ALWAYS—AND VIGOROUSLY—DISPUTED anybody who said he gave a speech. "(I)t wasn't a speech," Proctor told James Morrow in an interview in 1908 for the *Washington Post*.[170] He wrote Brooks at the time, "I thought that I made a very conservative mild statement of the situation, but it is charged upon me by the peace-at-any-price men that I am bringing on a war."[171] An illuminating fragment survives in the copybook version of this letter. Proctor had begun to write, "If a moderate statement of the facts" but then crossed it out. He concluded instead, "I incline to accept the charge with all its responsibility."[172] Proctor, who would not admit that he gave a speech, offered no opposition to a claim that whatever it was, it led to war. As noted, Proctor opted for the Senate aloud rather than the press room on paper because of Day. But it was Senator William Frye of Maine who made Proctor speak immediately on March 17. Frye was an ardent Cuban interventionist, perhaps the most ardent in all of Congress. Frye's insistence is strong circumstantial evidence that Proctor showed him his notes.[173]

---

[170] *Washington Post*. March 22, 1908, PFPL.

[171] Proctor to Brooks, March 29, 1898, Folder 38, 456, PFPL.

[172] Id.

[173] Neither Proctor nor Frye documented that Frye read his notes. The author so concludes as it is only logical that Frye would not have urgently insisted Proctor to speak (which he did by Proctor's account) without a good idea of what Proctor was to say.

Proctor protested feebly about wanting to type his draft as Frye led him through the Capitol. After Frye deposited Proctor in the Senate cloakroom, the dynamic Mainer got Florida's peppery Senator Mallory[174] to yield the floor in mid-speech.

At Proctor's memorial in 1908, Senator Perkins of California said that Proctor had told him he

> did not intend at that time to deliver as a speech that which he had written, but when he came into the Chamber he found there such a mass of expectant and breathless auditors, the newspaper press being also represented in the gallery and on the floor, that he was impelled to speak . . . he could not resist the temptation, and so he gave us the never-to-be-forgotten story of his trip.[175]

That audience of expectant and breathless senators was fictional. An immediate quorum call drummed up pathetically few members. Any hushed silence is best explained by empty seats. Of the ninety senators who represented the forty-five states of the Union, forty-six answered present, and that counts Frye and Proctor.[176] When Proctor began to speak, the Senate chamber remained half-empty.

Among the absent were leaders like Henry Cabot Lodge, Sr., the chairman of the Foreign Relations Committee, and Ohio's

---

[174] Mallory, born in 1848, enlisted in the Confederate Army in 1864, when he was just 16. In 1865, he served as a midshipman in the Confederate Navy. After the war, Mallory taught Greek and Latin before he practiced law in Louisiana and Florida. Upon turning to politics, he served first in the House before he became a Senator. http://bioguide.congress.gov/scripts/biodisplay.pl?index=M000085 (accessed 1/12/2009).

[175] Id., 35.

[176] *Cong. Rec.*, 55th Cong., 2nd sess., 1898.

non-interventionist Mark Hanna, who later told Proctor that, had he known, he would have gotten down on his knees and begged Proctor not to speak. Also absent were Senators Gallinger and Thurston, the two senators sent to Cuba officially. (Perhaps neither were in Washington, although Gallinger's impressions of Cuba had already been published in the newspapers.)

Senators familiar with Proctor's typical and unmemorable way with words may have winced to hear that Proctor was going to speak. Despite a deep bass voice[177] Proctor rarely spoke publicly. No lack of education explained it, as he was a college graduate, nor shyness, as he was an excellent salesman. It is speculative but remains possible that his lungs were so scarred during severe tuberculosis in 1862 that his body would not support the activity. On point, Andrew Delbanco characterized nineteenth century speechmaking as "a test of stamina that required the histrionic skills of an opera singer or a revival preacher."[178] When Proctor's son, Fletcher, wrote of his father as "affable and genial in conversation," he made no remark about public address skills. He praised instead his father's "broad and thorough research and reading."[179] Senator Dillingham summarized similarly that "his addresses indicated patient research, deep thought and strong convictions, and his grave and earnest spirit gave emphasis to his

[177] Partridge, 92. ("Senator Hoar once said jokingly in the course of a debate in the Senate that he had heard that a Vermonter was not permitted to vote until he had made a certain number of dollars out of a Massachusetts man in a horse trade, and Senator Proctor instantly interjected in his deep voice "And we all vote.") Also, James B. Morrow in an interview published posthumously by the *Washington Post*, Sunday, March 22, 1908, referred to Proctor as "deep-throated."

[178] Andrew Delbanco, "Lincoln's Sacramental Language," in Eric Foner, ed., Our Lincoln, New Perspectives on Lincoln and His World (New York: W.W. Norton & Co., 2008), 202.

[179] Partridge, 101.

utterances."[180] H.B.F. MacFarland,[181] having compared Proctor to Lincoln for his height and build, his long face and short beard, conscientiously added, "I do not say he has Lincoln's genius any more than he has Lincoln's eloquence, but he has, so to speak, the roots of both."[182]

But reporters ravenous for information about the *Maine* or, secondarily, about Cuba in general, had professional incentives to hope for something they might spin into a story. Besides the hopeful press, only one person in the Capitol seems to have been actually excited. That was non-interventionist Speaker of the House Reed, who dashed into the senate chamber to listen.

Following the disappointing quorum call, Frye introduced Proctor tidily as "a Senator in whom the country has much confidence, and a conservative man" who was going to share "a pretty careful investigation of affairs in Cuba."[183]

What followed was, indeed, no traditional speech. Proctor's presentation to the Senate on March 17, 1898, was more an unhurried recitation of notes. It was an unemotional recitation that comprised the single occasion that Proctor spoke with great, even national and explosive, effect.

Proctor did not do so by satisfying reporters who had written that Proctor went to Cuba for McKinley. And he did nothing for any reporter who hoped for a scoop about the *Maine*. Rather, he deflated any such expectations early. He began stating that his visit had no official character and that he had nothing to say about

---

[180] Id., 90.

[181] Then-chairman, Board of Commissioners, District of Columbia.

[182] Partridge, 100.

[183] *Cong. Rec.*, 55th Cong., 2nd sess., 1898.

the *Maine*. Speaker Reed did not then stay long.[184] But Proctor had only just begun to speak.

Moreover, the spectacle of the most silent of Senators reading notes charmed the press. The next day's *Chicago Tribune* explained to Mid-Westerners that the

> recognition of the independence of Cuba by President McKinley in the immediate future was distinctly foreshadowed by the remarkable address made by Senator Proctor. On all sides it is taken for granted that the Vermont Senator speaks by the card, and it is a well established fact that at least the outline and probably the exact text of the speech was submitted to the President and approved by him. Senator Proctor's relations with President McKinley have been so absolutely confidential that his associates in the Senate at once received the speech as an inspired declaration of the policy of the administration, especially intended to prepare the public mind for what the President is about to do.[185]

---

[184] Reed's absence from most of Proctor's recitation did not prevent reporters from later quoting him. Reed, whose Presidential aspirations Proctor had soured by boosting McKinley in Vermont, supposedly said that the marble baron's position was to be expected because "a war will make a large market for gravestones." Arthur Wallace Dunn, From Harrison to Harding, A Personal Narrative, Covering a Third of a Century 1888-1921 (New York: Putnam's, 1922), vol. 1, 234. The accuracy of this quote has always been suspect among scholars. See, e.g., Trask, The War with Spain (New York: Macmillan Publishing Co., Inc., 1981), n. 14, 504. The same scholars acknowledge Reed's cold relationship with Proctor, rendering the cutting remark a not completely implausible witticism.

[185] *Chicago Tribune*, March 18, 1898, 2.

Over his protest, Proctor's recitation was understood to be what McKinley wanted to be said. Its 52 paragraphs mostly (16 paragraphs) concerned conditions of the *reconcentrados.* Another eight paragraphs reported his surveillance of the Spanish military. Seven paragraphs of introductory remarks and seven on the political situation in Cuba made no news but his five paragraphs on the Red Cross were most important. Five other paragraphs on Cuban demographics were encyclopedia-style surplusage. Two paragraphs about his sources and two telling his fellow citizens that they, not he, must decide what to do next, rounded out his recitation.

Slowly and unemotionally, Proctor described "desolation and distress, misery and starvation"[186] facing *reconcentrados* in Cuba. From Proctor Americans learned of death on a scale they had not known since their own Civil War.[187] Proctor spoke of an unimaginable number: he estimated that 300,000 *reconcentrados* had died in two years, the product of death camps of civilians killed *en masse* by starvation and disease, mostly women, children and elderly. Proctor was just back from the places of greatest suffering in the world.

Of civilian suffering and deaths, Proctor admitted, "I went to Cuba with a strong conviction that the picture had been overdrawn."[188] He thought that journalists had exaggerated "a few cases of starvation and suffering" and circulated photographs of sick and starving *reconcentrados* that were atypical.[189]

"I saw plenty as bad or worse," Proctor said of the victims in photographs, recalling many from his trip "that should not be

[186] *Cong. Rec.*, 55th Cong., 2nd sess., 1898, 2916.

[187] See, e.g., Drew Gilpin Faust, This Republic of Suffering: death and the American Civil War, (New York: Alfred A. Knopf, 2008).

[188] Id., 2917.

[189] Id.

photographed and shown."[190] He spoke of emaciated women and children in hospitals "with the scantiest covering of rags—and such rags!"[191]

Almost incidentally, Proctor gave thought-provoking military figures, estimating that only 60,000 soldiers remained fit for duty of an original 200,000 sent from Spain.[192] According to Proctor, even the surviving troops were poorly-trained. Proctor offered reconnaissance to his fellow senators, "I saw no drills or regular formation."[193] Of cavalry, in a rare moment of humor Proctor mocked the Spaniards' "scrubby little native ponies, weighing not over 800 pounds, tough and hardy, but for the most part in wretched condition, reminding one of the mount of Don Quixote."[194]

Proctor the careful researcher, notes in hand, speaking simply, appeared to be an up-to-date, representative and reliable informant about Cuba. Cooley described Proctor as an orator who, when called upon to speak in Vermont, "aimed right for the point, as in debate, or turned to humor of a dry and rather self-conscious sort."[195] Proctor in Washington on March 17, 1898, stood and spoke as that same old Proctor.

Proctor had to address and did address what at that time seemed to be the only thing standing between peace and war with Spain, the Red Cross. The Red Cross posed a dilemma for

---

[190] Id.

[191] Id.

[192] *Cong. Rec.*, 55th Cong., 2nd sess., 1898, 2918. Proctor's confidence was statistically unfounded. The United States standing army of 25,000 numbered less than half of his figure of fit Spanish soldiers. And Proctor's estimate was wrong. There were about 150,000 Spanish troops ready in Cuba, better-armed than American soldiers at the time. Tone, 258. However, "McKinley's call for 125,000 volunteers produced over a million applicants." Id., 259.

[193] Id.

[194] *Cong. Rec.*, 55th Cong., 2nd sess., 1898, 2916.

[195] Memorial, 233.

Proctor because two friends of his, McKinley and Barton, had not alleviated ghastly conditions in such places as Matanzas, a city occupied by the dead and dying. Even in Havana thousands well enough to stand in line for Red Cross bread literally stood for uncounted numbers of relatives and friends who were unable even to walk.[196] By default of any other option, Proctor praised the efficiency of the Red Cross. He gave the highest compliment he could. He said that it was run like a business. But the hellish conditions all over Cuba he spoke of, along with his voucher that the Red Cross was distributing food and medicines "in the best possible manner,"[197] together spelled a catastrophe that the Red Cross at its most efficient, and the American public at its most charitable, could not deal with effectively. Hundreds of thousands of endangered women, children and elderly Cubans gave Proctor equanimity about war, and that equanimity was contagious.

Proctor said finally that "it is not my purpose at this time, nor do I consider it my province, to suggest any plan. I merely speak of the symptoms as I saw them, but do not undertake to prescribe. Such remedial steps as may be required may safely be left to an American President and the American people."[198] Proctor's position made people expect an imminent announcement from the White House.

The few senators present turned to one another. They hardly knew what to make of what they heard, essentially a report without a recommendation. They all distinguished a speech from a statement. The *New York Times* reporter heard and repeated

---

[196] Barton, 554-555, described prone figures on dank, dirty floors of "Los Fosos," an abandoned military garrison in sad disrepair. She eventually turned it into a clean and equipped hospital, but this was after Proctor's departure.

[197] *Cong. Rec.*, 55th Cong., 2nd sess., 1898, 2917

[198] *Cong. Rec.*, 55th Cong., 2nd sess., 1898, 2919.

their comments without attribution including, "A remarkable statement!" "A simple, straightforward statement of a horrible condition of affairs!" "A most effective and convincing statement!" "A temperate and timely utterance!"[199]

Senator Frye knew exactly what to emphasize: credibility. He told reporters, "It is just as if Proctor had held up his right hand and sworn to it."[200] Senator Chandler of New Hampshire, another interventionist, was no less satisfied. From the chair presiding over the senate, he jotted a note for Proctor which said, "God Bless You. Not A Word Could Be Changed."[201]

Proctor's statement, run in full as front page news, generated a firestorm. Editors elevated the Republican Party insider, friend and advisor of the President, a millionaire beholden to nobody, as one who in their reporters' presence and before congressional witnesses verified that stories of Spanish outrages in Cuba that they had run for years were true.

McKinley's silence fell under immediate siege. Patience expired as an option. For example, the *Omaha World Record* urged action and cursed the lukewarm. Its editorial said, "Humanity and justice demand action—now, now, now," and concluded, "The man who can keep cool as he reads Senator Proctor's report of starvation and misery in Cuba would freeze in Hades." The *Chicago Post* wanted to wipe away the "blood of innocents" on our doorstep. The *Boston Traveller* said that the "hands of dying mothers and little children stretch toward us in agony." The *Sacramento Bee* spoke of heeding "the cries of the starving Cubans."[202]

After Proctor's speech, only one newspaper, the *Rochester Times*, held tight to the McKinley-Barton line. That newspaper

---

[199] *New York Times*, March 18, 1898, 2.

[200] Leech, 172.

[201] Bowie, 373.

[202] All of these are from Bowie,.

evoked Clara Barton's first overseas success and equated Cuba with "an American Armenia less than 100 miles from our shores."[203]

The McKinley-Barton peace plan collapsed elsewhere. Businessmen formerly against of the risks of war told the *Wall Street Journal* that Proctor's speech "made the blood boil."[204] In its editorial, the *American Banker* pumped for intervention so that an "outraged people might be set free!"[205] The Chicago *Economist* opined more cautiously but with increasing militancy that war would not hurt business "or endanger the gold standard."[206]

Church newspapers switched to support intervention.[207] The degree and form of conversion varied but the timing did not. The Congregational *Advance* had denounced yellow journals before Proctor's speech, as late as March 10. Immediately after Proctor's speech, the March 24 issue of the *Advance* declared that American newspaper accounts were borne out and that Cubans deserved independence with American support. On Sunday, March 27,

---

[203] These five press quotations are from Bowie, 370-371.

[204] *Wall Street Journal*, March 19, 1898. Item quoted at greater length in Pratt, 246.

[205] *American Banker*, LXIII, 489 (March 23, 1898), quoted by Pratt, 247.

[206] *Economist*, March 19, 1898. Quoted by Pratt, 244. Pratt's conclusion that the American business community endorsed war in reaction to the spectacle of suffering Cuba remains controversial. Arthur Barcan, in an unpublished Master's thesis, "American Imperialism and the Spanish American War," Columbia University, 1940, a wider study of more business publications over a longer time-span, concluded that the American business community's interest in an Asian/Pacific market, i.e., Hawaii, Philippines, was constant and that its interest in Cuba only derived from a belated awareness of the Pacific consequences likely concomitant to a Cuban-inspired war. See also Marilyn Blatt Young, American Expansionism, The Critical Issues, (Boston: Little, Brown and Co., 1973), esp. essay by Philip S. Foner, "Why the United States Went to War with Spain in 1898," beginning at p. 6.

[207] Julius W. Pratt, Expansionists of 1898: The Acquisition of Hawaii and the Spanish Islands (Baltimore: The Johns Hopkins Press, 1936), 284, 288.

1898, a Brooklyn minister discounted differences about the *Maine*. Ignoring the imminent *Maine* report, he told parishioners, "I say that when men and women and children are being starved to death in Cuba peace is unholy. I am a minister of peace but such peace is not a Christian peace."[208] The *Catholic Herald* had favored papal arbitration between Spain and Cuba, but on April 9 stated that if it came to war, American Catholics would do their duty as patriotic citizens.

Senators whom the *New York Times* reporter had quoted for mild "Remarkable speech!" exclamations were succeeded by spokesmen like former President Benjamin Harrison. Harrison opined superlatively that there had not been made "in any legislative assembly of the world in fifty years a speech that so powerfully affected public sentiment."[209] Catching up, the *New York Times* featured Proctor's formal portrait on the cover of its Sunday magazine on April 3, 1898, above the caption, "Redfield Proctor, United States Senator from Vermont, who told us the plain truth about Cuba."[210]

Outside the country, Proctor's words were taken as a signal. Within two weeks, in Madrid, McKinley's minister Stewart L. Woodford told Prime Minister Sagasta

> that the sober sense of the American people insisted upon immediate cessation of hostilities; that we could not wait until the Cuban congress should meet; that practical and effective peace must come now, and at once. In this connection I referred to the

---

[208] *New York Times*, March 28, 1898, 3. The minister was Reverend Dr. Ferdinand C. Iglehart of the Methodist Episcopal Church.

[209] Joseph Wisan, The Cuban Crisis as reflected in the New York Press, 1895-1898 (New York: Octagon Books, 1934), n. 90, 412.

[210] *New York Times*, magazine supplement, April 4, 1898.

> recent speech of Senator Proctor. I said that I knew Senator Proctor well; that he had been a member of President Harrison's cabinet; that he is one of the most conservative and reliable of our public men, and that after his public and serious statement I could no longer conscientiously consent, on the part of my Government, to the slightest delay in securing immediate and effective peace.[211]

Woodford's citation to Proctor is surreal, given Proctor's emphatic rejection of the role of the prescriber of action on Cuba.

When, on March 21, 1898, the Navy announced that the inquiry board's report was complete, the country's openness to new information about Cuba had passed. Neither McKinley nor the country was in any rush. Unhurriedly, the now-anti-climactic report sailed from Cuba to Florida, then up the coast by train to Washington, from Union Station by carriage to a hotel overnight on March 24, 1898. On Friday morning, March 25, 1898, its military couriers delivered it in hand at the White House. McKinley took the weekend to review it before he submitted it to Congress on March 28, 1898.

During this time after Proctor's speech and before the *Maine* report, Senator Thurston spoke on March 24, 1898 about his official visit to Cuba. His wife, one of the "court ladies" of the Red Cross, had died in Cuba during their trip there together. Thurston delivered a thrilling, patriotic speech. It was vigorously cheered by packed galleries. He ended with a narration of his wife's dedication to the cause of the *reconcentrados*, then collapsed into sobbing at his desk. Contrary to all precedent, the galleries' reaction was not gaveled down by the chair. Run in full by newspapers, Thurston's

[211] *Foreign Relations* (1898), 723-724.

speech added nothing to the national dialogue, nor did Gallinger's similarly rousing speech later.

In contrast to Thurston's and Gallinger's stem-winders, what explains the spontaneous and astonishingly intense national reaction to Proctor's recitation of travel notes? Proctor did not deliver his report with any emotion. His statement reflected a typical plodding Proctor delivery. Professor Joseph Wisan said that Proctor's "dispassionate and sincere manner, added to the effect,"[212] but that effect was not contrived or exceptional. Like Wisan, Senator Dillingham found effect in Proctor's "cold, bare, plain statement" such that "the facts stated burned themselves into the minds of every Senator present, and, being heralded by the press, roused the nation to action."[213] Proctor's long-time friend and Vermont political aid, Frank Partridge, suggested in the alternative, "Its observations were wise because he was always a wise observer. Its style was simple and direct because such was always his manner."[214]

On the other hand, Proctor was both a Civil War veteran and former Secretary of War. He could offer military expertise possessed by no other speaker when he held Spain's military forces in derision. Newspapers carried his derogatory evaluation of the Spanish military along with his first-hand report about the Red Cross and the desperate condition of the Cubans. Americans who learned that the *reconcentrados* were still suffering and dying understood also that the *reconcentrados* were guarded by badly-trained and poorly-equipped soldiers with cavalry ponies like Don Quixote's nag. If the Red Cross was not enough, it seemed inexcusable not to send the *reconcentrados* rescuers of a different sort.

---

212 Wisan, 412.

213 Memorial, 18.

214 Partridge, 92.

As such logical deductions were made in homes, on Wall Street, in churches and in editorial rooms of the country's newspapers, Proctor confronted McKinley for the first time after his speech. The meeting probably took place at the White House, which McKinley rarely left. It probably happened on the first day of spring. Cortelyou documented that Proctor was among McKinley's visitors on March 21, 1898. Although Proctor never recounted what McKinley did or said to precipitate his defensive remark, but an implication that McKinley revealed displeasure is clear enough.

"You know . . . that I did not promise to withhold the statement,"[215] Proctor remembered himself saying, imploring McKinley to recollect.

"That is true," McKinley said but McKinley then tipped his hand and revealed his original intention when he added, "But I thought you would wait. I wanted Senator Hoar to read what you had written."[216]

Proctor, the newly-confident national spokesman on Cuba, bristled. He growled, "I have a very high opinion of Hoar but I am not in the habit of consulting him as to what I shall say."[217]

Ironically, Hoar was one of the Senators most touched by Proctor's speech. "(I)t was what led me to give my consent in the end to the declaration (of war)," Hoar wrote a friend.[218] The dove

---

[215] Linderman, 56.

[216] Id.

[217] Id.

[218] G.F. Hoar to Edward Atkinson, September 2, 1898, Atkinson Papers, Massachusetts Historical Society. ("I suppose (Proctor's) picture of the misery and starvation . . . was in the main true, and that it was that picture which brought about the war. Certainly it was what led me to give my consent in the end to the declaration (of war)." Quoted in Richard E. Welch, Jr., George Frisbie Hoar and the Half-Breed Republicans, (Cambridge: Harvard University Press, 1971), n. 28, 215.

became a hawk. Hoar echoed Proctor before McKinley did. Hoar rose to address the Senate on April 14, saying that stopping the deliberate starvation of thousands of human beings necessitated military intervention.[219] Two days before that speech, Hoar had written William Claflin, "(W)e cannot look idly while . . . innocent human beings, women, children and old men, die of hunger close to our doors."[220]

---

[219] *Cong. Rec.,* 55th Congress, 2d session, 3832-3835.

[220] G.F. Hoar to William Claflin, April 12, 1898, Claflin Papers, Rutherford B. Hayes Library, quoted in Welch, 214.

Chapter 8

McKINLEY ECHOES PROCTOR

PROCTOR SPOKE DURING A LONG period of renewed Presidential silence about Cuba. Upon receiving the cablegram at the White House that the *Maine* had sunk, McKinley had the Secretary of the Navy issue an announcement that the Navy would be investigating the cause of the loss and for the country to remain calm.[221] For forty days thereafter only a privileged few met and spoke with McKinley. Among them, as McKinley and the country waited for the Navy's report, were Charles G. Dawes and George Cortelyou. Equally important to historians, both men kept diaries.

Wealthy Dawes lived near the White House in a house noted for "its stable of good horses."[222] Cortelyou, a former teacher still paying off debts from his failed experimental private school, was a stenographer, a courier and overseer of White House copyists. Dawes, an early McKinley campaigner,[223] had been awarded the position of Comptroller of Currency[224] by the President. Their relationship was as close as "father and son."[225] Cortelyou was all business and Presidencies were his business. Dawes lunched at the White House, played cards and rode a carriage with McKinley.

---

[221] "Judgment should be suspended until a full investigation is made." Gould, 35.

[222] Dawes, xvi.

[223] Id., ix-xi.

[224] Id., xiii.

[225] Id., xvi. (Foreword by editor, Bascom N. Timmons.)

McKinley spent the last hour of each day mainly dictating or discussing correspondence with Cortelyou. [226]

Cortelyou's diary entries on March 17, 1898 contain nothing about Proctor's speech. Cortelyou described that McKinley showed him news from Madrid, two cables from Woodford. One was only the latest installment of a series of exchanges on Lee's acceptability as consul in Havana. The other communicated Spanish concern that "sending relief supplies in naval vessels was calculated to cause serious embarrassment."[227] McKinley discerned a threat to his peace plan. Hours after Proctor's speech on starving Cubans, McKinley gave Cortelyou strict orders. He was to bring the cables to Day the next morning. McKinley stressed, "Keep these in your own hands, do not let them pass through any hands but your own."[228] The next day, Friday, March 18, "at about 2:45 (p.m.), Judge Day came over to remain with the President both before and after the regular Friday afternoon recreation."[229] Day escorted his wife, Mrs. McKinley and others to a play while the President continued to work. When Day and the ladies returned, Cortelyou was present. McKinley had them come into the cabinet room and

---

[226] Ford, 43. According to Ford, Cleveland told McKinley, "Whatever changes you make in your office force, hang onto Cortelyou." McKinley did. Uniquely, Cortelyou served three very different men, Presidents from both political parties, a one-man "transition team" whom Theodore Roosevelt retained in his turn. As soon as he could T.R. brought Cortelyou into his cabinet as Postmaster General. Insider Cortelyou may have reminisced with McKinley about Cleveland's successful policy of selective silence during the Venezualan crisis, a silence interrupted only by increasingly bellicose statements. Or any resemblance between McKinley's Cuban strategy and Cleveland's Venezualan strategy may be purely coincidental. Lewis Gould titled the first chapter of his exploration of the evolution of the American Presidency through the Twentieth Century "The Age of Cortelyou."

[227] Cortelyou Diary, LC, March 17, 1898.

[228] Id.

[229] Id., March 18, 1898.

"read to them some of the letters he was receiving from different parts of the country, notably one from an old gentleman who commended his firm policy and his determination to wait until convinced that he was right before going ahead."[230]

McKinley lived for such public support. On Saturday, March 19, Dawes recorded in his diary that McKinley, whom he saw as perpetually cheerful, was in "better spirits than usual."[231] On the same date Dawes wrote, "If war comes it will be because the starvation and suffering in Cuba is such that the United States orders it stopped upon grounds of humanity and outraged justice, and that order of intervention is resisted by Spain."[232]

From another source we know that on March 19, Oscar Straus, a New York businessman, advised McKinley about "suzerainty," face-saving or technical sovereignty. Straus explained that Egypt was the recipient of tribute in the form of customs money from its self-governing subjects in Turkey.[233] McKinley complained to Straus, "We will have great trouble in satisfying the insurgents or in getting them to agree to anything—they are even more difficult than Spain to deal with."[234]

The country's reception was immediately instructive. Any politician who wanted to know what Americans wanted to hear suddenly needed no other data. Mute President McKinley, although he soon and angrily confronted Proctor, within a month recaptured public approval by copying him. In his so-called "war message" to Congress on April 11, 1898 McKinley referred only in passing to the *Maine*. He tracked Proctor's theme of a humanitarian crisis. Further, McKinley mimicked Proctor's eyewitness account. There was only one way he could. He released accounts of the Cuban holocaust sent

---

230 Id.

231 Dawes, 148.

232 Id., 147.

233 Gould, 76.

234 Id.

to Washington by the five American consuls in various provinces of the island. These Cuban consular correspondences, secret until the President's message, were made available to every newspaper. Long, shocking excerpts were run alongside McKinley's own message, making each newspaper an echo of Proctor's March 17 speech.

McKinley's audience, of course, already stood persuaded. Proctor had spoken. Among others, Massachusetts Senator George Frisbie Hoar, a very reluctant interventionist, credited Proctor's speech specifically as determining his "yea" vote for war with Spain. We remember the *Maine* better than we remember Proctor but his speech and the spectacle of its reception can yet be reconstructed. The connection once clear to millions between Proctor's speech and the beginning of the War of 1898 is recovered here.

Telling about the genesis of national popular support for war with Spain or merely the story of McKinley's April 11 message to Congress requires telling about Proctor. Ironically, the Cuban question had no great significance to Proctor until 1898. His trip to Cuba remained unlikely up to the night he left Washington, three days after the *Maine* exploded. Likewise, his speech remained improbable until the morning of the day he delivered it. But his speech was so well-received that, two weeks later, he dared to advise McKinley on what to say to Congress about Cuba. As his country and McKinley wrestled with war and peace, Proctor played a key role. In short, during the country's and McKinley's struggle, Proctor guided both.

Even the war's earliest historians gave Proctor little attention. For example, Proctor's colleague, Senator Henry Cabot Lodge, Sr., a former Harvard history professor, as a senator continued to write histories. The *Maine*-elevating theory Lodge espoused has since become standard. Lodge wrote that when the *Maine* went down a "wave of fierce wrath swept over the American people."[235]

---

[235] Henry Cabot Lodge, The War with Spain (New York: Harper & Brothers Publishers, 1899), 29.

Although Proctor spoke on March 17, 1898, Lodge wrote that "(s) carcely a word was said in either House or Senate, and for forty days the American people and the American Congress waited in silence for the verdict of the board of naval officers who had been appointed to report on the destruction of the *Maine*."[236] According to Lodge, the climactic event was the report on the *Maine*, when the "peace-at-any-price people fought hard but in vain against the sweeping tide of public sentiment."[237] But a vestige of the truth remains imbedded in Lodge's history. Proctor's photograph appears in his history book over a caption that Proctor's "report of his observations of the results of Spanish rule in Cuba profoundly influenced public feeling in America."[238]

By contrast, another of the war's first historians allowed Proctor more. Henry B. Russell wrote that Proctor's speech made a "more marked impression upon Congress and the country" than anything else between the explosion of the *Maine* and the declaration of war.[239] Specifically, Russell said that when Proctor

> described in cool, dispassionate language the conditions of Cuba as he saw them in February and early in March, and voiced his judgment concerning the future of Cuba if it continued under Spanish rule, . . . doubtful people began to realize why it was that so many had long urged intervention. He assured the Senate that he spoke without any consultation with the President, and that his words could only be interpreted as an

---

[236] Id.

[237] Id., 33. In Lodge's account, intervention was largely guided by the Senate Foreign Relations Committee, which Lodge chaired.

[238] Id., photograph opposite page 40.

[239] Henry B. Russell, An Illustrated History of Our War with Spain: Its Causes, Incidents and Results, (Hartford, Connecticut: A.D. Worthington & Co., Publ., 1898), 446. The book runs 780 pages.

> expression of his personal belief, but it was well known that he was a close friend of the President, and that his judgment was prized at the White House.[240]

Despite his cameo appearance in Senator Lodge's history and the account in Russell's book, Proctor's historical importance ebbed as attention drifted toward the battleship. Well-informed lay persons observed and criticized the trend. Lyman Abbott wrote in his memoirs that

> the Spanish American War has been often attributed to the destruction of the *Maine*... In fact, that destruction took place February 15, and war was not declared until April 24, more than two months later. The real occasion of the war was the report of Senator Proctor of Vermont . . . ; it aroused in the country a storm of humanitarian indignation which proved irresistible.[241]

---

[240] Id., 446. As to Proctor and President McKinley, Proctor was a close friend and valued advisor of the President. As to consultation, Proctor revealed years later that he had gone to the White House with his notes, which McKinley read before giving him a nod to release his words.

[241] Lyman Abbott, Reminiscences (Boston, Houghton Mifflin, 1915), 436-437, quoted in Michelle Bray Davis and Rollin W. Quimby, "Senator Proctor's Cuban Speech: Speculations on a Cause of the Spanish-American War," *Quarterly Journal of Speech* 55 (April 1969), 131. Curiously, Abbott, a social activist/clergyman with a pulpit in Brooklyn, gave a sermon in favor of free Cuba on the Sunday before Proctor's speech. Wilkerson, 110. (cited in the *New York Journal*, March 14, 1898, 1.) The sinking of the *Maine* alone obviously sufficed to stir Abbott to take a position. But given Abbott's vantage-point in New York City, a hotbed for pro-Cuba partisans, which he already attempted to arouse, his support for Proctor's priority implies a responsiveness which he did not detect in strength until after March 17.

Academic scholars discerned Proctor's historical significance. William Karraker boldly declared that Proctor's speech was the "prime factor responsible for the precipitation of the War with Spain" in his Ph.D. dissertation in 1940.[242] Karraker's characterization languished without a second until Professor Gerald F. Linderman, more than thirty years later, in 1974 in his study of the War of 1898, devoted a chapter to Proctor's role. Recently, in his own panoramic survey, Professor Paul T. McCartney wrote that "after Senator Proctor's speech, the possibility of war was too great to ignore."[243] McCartney summarized from primary sources that "in the public demonstrations, pamphlets, and petitions to Congress that provided the primary impetus for war, the American people clamored not for territorial conquest but for the relief of a brutally oppressed people living at the nation's doorstep."[244]

In his entry for Sunday, March 20, Cortelyou said, "The mail was heavy today as usual. The letters of advice and commendation continue to pour in."[245] More important, a confidential cable came through: Admiral Sampson's board was unanimous that the *Maine* had been blown up by a submarine mine. After McKinley consulted with Day, they decided to send new instructions to Woodford. The *Maine* incident could be settled by reparation but the President would put the Cuban question to Congress if Spain

---

[242] William A. Karraker, "The American Churches and the Spanish-American War," (unpublished Ph.D. dissertation, Divinity School, University of Chicago, 1940), 44, quoted in Michelle Bray Davis and Rollin W. Quimby, "Senator Proctor's Cuban Speech: Speculations on a Cause of the Spanish-American War," *Quarterly Journal of Speech* 55, (April 1969), 131.

[243] Paul T. McCartney, Power and Progress, American National Identity, the War of 1898, and the Rise of American Imperialism (Baton Rouge: Louisiana State University Press, 2006), 106.

[244] Id., 87.

[245] Cortelyou, LC, March 20, 1898. In his entry for March 22 Cortelyou said that "nearly half" of McKinley's mail was about Cuba.

did not take certain steps to correct "general conditions in Cuba which can not be longer endured, and which will demand action on our part."[246] That same Sunday in New York City at Madison Square Garden, Dwight L. Moody, the famed evangelist, began a mass meeting by reading Proctor's speech in its entirety. Then Moody slowly surveyed all attending and boomed, "I want every man and every woman to read that speech."[247]

After Proctor's speech Day and McKinley looked to Madrid for movement. McKinley said in a cable to Woodford about armistice and arbitration on March 19 that "April 15 is none too early date for accomplishment of these purposes."[248] He wanted Woodford to tell that to Sagasta. In other words, McKinley wanted Spain to end a three-year civil war and commence negotiations in less than one month.

On Monday, March 21, Cortelyou noted that McKinley interrupted a conference he was having with Senator Proctor and several other members of Congress in the cabinet room to show Speaker Reed to the White House library.[249] McKinley kept Reed, who had supposedly quipped that the "marble baron's" speech would create a good market for gravestones,[250] a discreet distance away from Proctor.

The Congressional majority McKinley had boasted of to de Loma at the diplomatic dinner in late January was melting away. His anti-war front line, Reed and Cannon in the House, Nelson

---

[246] Gould, 78.

[247] Partridge, 91-92.

[248] Gould, 78.

[249] Cortelyou, LC, March 21, 1898.

[250] Trask, 36. Trask believes that "A war will make a large market for gravestones," may be apocryphal while Leech, 172, quoted it with seeming confidence.

Aldrich, Oliver Pratt, William Allison and Mark Hanna in the Senate,[251] was crumbling.

McKinley, not completely without hope, continued to speak with Spain. Day later blamed Spain for the war. More specifically, Day later told John Bassett Moore[252] that "for any diplomatic history of the war to be intelligible, it should discuss the conditions in Cuba and the failure of Spain to better them."[253] Day, no less than McKinley, ignored the extent to which "conditions in Cuba" resulted from roving guerrillas.

McKinley thus remained sanguine. On March 22 he told Dawes over a game of euchre that he expected the suffering in Cuba to stop without war, and that only "broader grounds than the question of responsibility for the disaster to the *Maine*"[254] could justify military intervention. Sensing the right moment, John J. McCook, a New York attorney associated with the Cuban Junta,[255] sent a cover letter asking McKinley "whether the time has arrived for the immediate recognition of the Republic of Cuba" over a gratuitous legal memorandum of European precedents for military intervention, mostly citing Walker's Manual of Public International Law, i.e., "on the ground of humanity, in order to stay the effusion of blood," or "to put a stop to piracy and anarchy."[256]

---

[251] Phillips, 91. (Lists these as McKinley's staunch supporters "at least through March 1898.")

[252] John Bassett Moore was a gifted and versatile intellectual. In 1898 he had just completed a six-volume history of international arbitration, the first of seven works on international relations which he would author while holding the chair of international law and diplomacy at Columbia. Moore had preceded Day as Assistant Secretary of State 1886-1891. Day corresponded with Moore, seeking opinions and advice beginning in 1897.

[253] Phillips, 95, citing Morgan, *America's Road to Empire*, 60.

[254] Dawes, 147.

[255] Offner, 128.

[256] McKinley correspondence, Library of Congress, Film 922, Microfilm Reel 3 (12/24/1897-6/23/1898).

McKinley was unready for any such intervention. He remained focused on food for peace. On Saturday, March 26, Dawes learned that McKinley planned to send the naval board report to Congress on Monday followed on Tuesday by a request for an appropriation to feed the starving in Cuba. Dawes wrote with admiration and approval that "he will feed these people whether Spain objects or not."[257] At the same time Cortelyou "marveled at the President's firmness, and especially his refusal to be pushed or rattled by the jingoists."[258]

John Bassett Moore, an expert in international law on emergency leave to the government from Columbia, said that he "first met Judge Day perhaps about a month before the outbreak of the war."[259] He, thus, may have had a hand in late March developments. Among these, McKinley wired Woodford on Sunday, March 27.[260] He told Woodford that he could not look upon "the suffering and starvation in Cuba save with horror . . . There has been no relief to the starving except such as the American people have supplied."[261] He set two goals: "Armistice until October 1. Negotiations meantime looking for peace between Spain and insurgents through friendly offices of President United States."[262]

On the night of March 27 McKinley "dictated very rapidly" to Cortelyou a brief message to go to Congress along with the naval inquiry's report on the *Maine*, released to Congress and the country the next day.

---

[257] Dawes, 148.

[258] Ford, 55.

[259] McLean, 32. Bassett characterized Day once generally as "wise enough to seek the advice of those who had experience" in diplomacy. Id., 36, n. 17. He was not more specific.

[260] Olcott, II, 19.

[261] Id., 20.

[262] Gould, 79.

On the same day in Ohio, one of McKinley's extended family, Russell Hastings,[263] wrote a letter that began "My dear Major." Hastings said that "Senator Proctor's report seems to have solidified all elements." He urged his relative to "put a stop to such barbarity and the quicker the better."[264]

On Monday, March 28, McKinley dictated a lengthy follow-up message, a draft for Congress. That week[265] Proctor wrote an undated letter of advice to McKinley. At the letter's top upper left someone wrote and then underlined "File Strictly Confidential." It began "Dear Mr. President" and followed:

> I have kept away from you because I do not wish to add a feather's weight to your labors & not from any lack of interest in them or in you, for nothing else is in my mind. The evening paper & Capitol rumors speak of your favoring "intervention" & opposing "recognition"—Now, why favor or oppose either? Why not after stating the facts place the matter in the hands of Congress, stating earnestly that whatever action they take will be put in execution with all the powers at your command? Such a statement would

[263] According to Leech, Hastings was "a one-legged veteran of the war and the dearest of McKinley's comrades." Leech, 20. Some twenty years earlier, in a courtship encouraged by Mrs. McKinley, Hastings married happily. He and the niece of President Hayes exchanged vows in a White House wedding. Id.

[264] McKinley correspondence, Library of Congress, Film 922, Reel 3 (12/24/1897-6/23/1898).

[265] This document was sent to the author courtesy of Karl Ash, Archivist at the McKinley Presidential Library, from its collection of McKinley correspondence for 1898. The letter is not dated except as "Tuesday." It refers to Proctor's not having seen McKinley in a while. Proctor's visit to McKinley on Monday, March 21, 1898, is documented in Cortelyou's diary. The letter seems to have been written on Tuesday, March 29, 1898.

> do good at this time, would strengthen you & help unite & hold together all shades. I want to see you lead the columns & that is immensely important. It far outbalances the strong legal points against recognition of the present Cuban regime. There are some & I fear many who will say it is too late to throw any cloud over their title to recognition; that this organization to sustain which Gomez has fought & Marti & Maceo fell(,) has been recognized by the God of battles & in the hearts of the people.

McKinley's concern over public harmony bordered on obsession. Proctor rang that bell in his letter:

> It gives great chances for talk & I fear the opening of the floodgates & a division of sentiment.

Without pause, Proctor offered an ingenious solution:

> If you say nothing about recognition or intervention, merely say that Spanish sovereignty must cease (possibly that the Cuban people be free)[266] & leave the methods to Congress any difference about these will not affect you or your control of the situation. Many do not like the word "intervention" & think it may mean delay. The legal objections to recognition are well understood & will doubtless be fully stated in Congress, so there is less occasion for you to discuss it. Most everyone knows which he favors. Now it doesn't matter half as much whether we intervene

[266] Originally "Spanish sovereignty must cease & the Cuban people be free," Proctor added parentheses and the phrase "possibly that."

> or acknowledge their[267] independence as it does that what you say shall give Congress & the people no chances to differ with or get away from you.

Not done advising, Proctor mingled advice with prediction:

> Whatever expression is used the result will be the same. Spain will get off or be pushed off the Island & the Cuban people will recognize the Government that has carried on then & until they choose to form another. I might say much more but I spare you. If you give me any credit for being a fair judge of what will suit the "plain people," who are always right, it is in the line of the above rather than by favoring intervention or recognition—Give us a little "buncombe."[268] It is allowable on such an occasion. Credit me with a deep personal interest in you & all that concerns you as my excuse for this letter.[269]

In the White House the balance shifted from peace to war on Thursday, March 31. Deaf old Alvey Adee, a lifelong servitor of the State Department, was stationed at a telegraph line newly installed in the White House itself. Late that night, he flipped through his copy of the State Department cipher book to translate Woodford's long coded cable. McKinley was jolted out of any lingering sense

---

[267] Originally, "acknowledge independence," Proctor first inserted between and above these two words "that," then struck out "that" and squeezed in "their."

[268] "Buncombe" is a word that has Congressional roots. An 1845 North Carolina Congressman from Buncombe County "defended an irrelevant speech by claiming he was speaking to Buncombe." Merriam-Webster dictionary entry for "buncombe."

[269] McKinley Presidential Library, Canton, Ohio, courtesy of Archivist Karl Ash.

of momentum toward peace. Spain had not accepted the idea of an armistice. Nor would it countenance McKinley as arbitrator. A unilateral cessation of hostilities was no news. The Spaniards would not fire unless fired upon but the insurgents were still going to fight. The civil war would not end. *Reconcentrados* would still die. As April began, McKinley and Day realized that they had run out of time.[270] Day was the first to confide his changing sentiments. Assistant Secretary of the Navy Theodore Roosevelt was the recipient of Day's comment. Roosevelt wrote a friend on April 5 that Day, who Roosevelt thought was an advocate of peace under almost any conditions, "just told (him) that he had given up and that the President seems making up his mind to the same effect."[271]

But what would McKinley say? McKinley had to say something to Americans who had last heard from him about Cuba through his Secretary of State's press release on Christmas Eve, 1897. McKinley knew what the people wanted to hear. He knew how Proctor's speech had been received. Accordingly, McKinley changed the legalistic message of historical precedents that he had begun planning on March 16, the evening before Proctor spoke. On that night "much interested in the communications relating to the Cuban situation,"[272] McKinley had asked Cortelyou "to

---

[270] John Offner identified Aril 1, 1898 as the date on which the McKinley Administration decided to intervene militarily in Cuba in his article, "President McKinley's Final Attempt to Avoid War with Spain," 94 Ohio History 125, basically because the eminently datable event of McKinley's receipt of Woodford's cablegram on March 31. Offner's article reprises the first ten days of April, throughout which negotiations continued although the United States was at the brink of war. The entire article may be accessed athttp://publications.ohiohistory.org/ohstemplate.cfm?action=detail&Page=0094125.html&St . . . (accessed 6/1/2008).

[271] McLean, 38, n. 21, which cited Bishop, I, 90.

[272] Cortelyou, LC, March 16, 1898.

ascertain . . . when Texas was recognized by this country—when the United States recognized the independence of Texas."[273] Cortelyou understood that McKinley thought that the Texas recognition process would bear a very decisive role in answering current questions.[274] McKinley's ultimate message to Congress dealt with Texas only vestigially.[275]

In place of Texas McKinley listed four reasons to intervene in Cuba, namely:

(1) for humanity's sake and to end the devastation of Cuba,
(2) to protect American citizens and rights in the island,
(3) to end the dangers to both Cuban and American commerce, and
(4) to guarantee American strategic rights in the hemisphere[276]

The *Maine* did not make McKinley's list except indirectly under his second item.

Senator Henry Cabot Lodge, Sr., recalled that the President's April 11 message to Congress,[277] some 7,000 words read aloud by a clerk, was "listened to with intense interest and in profound silence, broken only by a wave of applause when the sentence was read which said, 'In behalf of humanity, in the name of civilization, in behalf of endangered American interests which give us the right and duty to speak and to act, the war in Cuba

---

[273] Id.

[274] Id.

[275] McKinley's message carried a narrative of the legal sparring which preceded recognition of Texas and of President Grant's decision not to recognize the Cuban revolutionaries during his administration.

[276] H. Wayne Morgan, America's Road to Empire, The War with Spain and Overseas Expansion (New York: Wiley, 1965), 62.

[277] Gould, 84. The President's message was read aloud by a clerk.

must stop.'"[278] House members clapped "only briefly and in a perfunctory manner."[279] Lodge said:

> The President led up to this declaration by a dispassionate review of the Cuban question, and by a strong and moving description of the conditions of the island, which he characterized as a wilderness and a grave. He asked Congress to empower him to end hostilities in Cuba, and to secure the establishment of a stable government, capable of maintaining order and observing its international obligations.[280]

McKinley wanted to secure "a full and final termination of hostilities between the Government of Spain and the people of Cuba" and "a stable government capable of maintaining order and observing its international obligations." Plainly, the *insurrectos* were no such government.

Although a majority in both houses would likely have quickly voted for recognition, neither Proctor in March nor the President in April suggested it, nor an ultimatum or a deadline for Spain to end hostilities or care adequately for the *reconcentrados* by a particular time on penalty of military intervention, even though McKinley had been issuing deadlines for Woodford to communicate in Madrid.

With his message on April 11 McKinley had State Department release the Cuban consular correspondences.[281] Thus, when editors received McKinley's speech they also received more horrifying and graphic facts about suffering *reconcentrados*. Selections from the

---

[278] Lodge, 35.

[279] Offner, 182, citing the *Washington Post* and Secretary Long's journal.

[280] Id.

[281] Offner, 183.

Cuban consular correspondences, 60,000 previously-unpublished eyewitness words from five American consuls, were printed in headlined columns beside the President's April 11 message.[282] Over McKinley's name, the whole Washington output of April 11 was a variation of Proctor's themes and evidence of suffering humanity. Offner highlighted the significance of these "large excerpts from the reports, which contributed to the public insistence that Spain leave Cuba."[283] Outdoing Proctor, the consular reports actually covered more of Cuba over a longer period. The consuls in Havana (Lee), Matanzas (Brice), Cienfuegos (McGarr), Santiago (Hyatt), and Sagua la Grande (Barker) had sent altogether some 60,000 words to Washington memorializing the plight of Cuban civilians.[284] Newspapers characterized the consuls as "impartial reporters"[285] whose reports every American was duty-bound to read.[286] Ironically, the inflammatory reports had been gathered, redacted and copied long before the *Maine* had exploded.[287] But because McKinley withheld them, the audience for Proctor's speech was not jaded.

McKinley quixotically recommended to Congress "in the interest of humanity and to aid in preserving the lives of the starving people of the island . . . that the distribution of food and supplies be continued and that an appropriation be made out of

---

[282] For example, the *Chicago Tribune*, April 12, 1898, 9, ran nearly a full page from the consular correspondences, including a large black-bordered summary of points drawn from them printed in boldface.

[283] Id.

[284] *New York Times*, April 12, 6.

[285] *Chicago Tribune*, April 12, 1898, 9.

[286] *New York Times*, April 12, 1898, 8.

[287] Id., 6.

the public Treasury to supplement the charity of our citizens."[288] But McKinley was charity's last advocate. The Red Cross line could not hold after Proctor's report and projection. Within two weeks, on April 25, 1898, Congress declared war on Spain.

Although McKinley copied Proctor in theme, in unemotional format, in vague agenda for action, and in detailed factuality through the simultaneously-released Cuban consular correspondences, nobody seems to have noticed the rhetorical echo. This is especially striking given his last paragraph. Even were one not to know that it followed lines literally recommended by Proctor, the resemblance to Proctor's conclusion was hard for anyone to miss. McKinley concluded, "The issue is now with the Congress. It is a solemn responsibility. I have exhausted every effort to relieve the intolerable condition of affairs which is at our doors. Prepared to execute any obligation imposed upon me by the Constitution and the law, I await your action."

The President disappointed about half of Congress but surging grassroots support saved McKinley's political stature. Speaking about McKinley's April 11 message, Gould summarized that both the press and the White House mail showed "a broadly based support for what McKinley had done."[289] Congress and at least some newspapers were initially contrary. Under the headline, "An Angry Congress," the *New York Times* summarized McKinley's message accurately but acerbically:

---

[288] Ironically, one scholar found in this McKinley's dark side. John Dobson, Reticent Expansionism, The Foreign policy of William McKinley, (Pittsburgh: Duquesne University Press, 1988), 63, suggests from his reading of Dawes' journal that McKinley was no idealist but, rather, he requested a special appropriation for Cuban relief intending to send food with or without Spanish approval. Then, if war came, it would come from Spain's interference with a humanitarian relief mission.

[289] Gould, 86.

> The President yesterday presented his Cuban message to Congress. It does not declare for Cuban independence nor disclose that in the negotiations with Spain this country ever has demanded that Cuba be freed from Spanish rule. It does not urge immediate armed intervention in behalf of the Cubans.
>
> It says the war in Cuba must be brought to an end and asks authority from Congress for the President to use the army and navy for the purpose of establishing a stable Government in Cuba capable of maintaining order and observing its international obligations. It also asks that an appropriation be made to carry on the work of caring for the starving people of Cuba.[290]

Proctor's durable structure sheltered McKinley from any widespread criticism. Both Dawes and Cortelyou, from their respective vantage points, discerned relief. As Congressmen groused,[291] Dawes went with his family to attend "the annual 'egg rolling' in the White House yards. A great crowd was present. The President seemed better, and relieved that his message had been sent in."[292] When conscientious Cortelyou analyzed incoming letters to McKinley after April 11 he found "not many of the critical kind."[293]

The stone that the builders rejected was the cornerstone of a new national determination. Gould summarized that McKinley's message "succeeded in establishing the terms of the debate by

---

[290] *New York Times*, April 12, 1898, 1.

[291] Senator Lodge wrote a friend on April 15, 1898, "Congress . . . has been compelled to strike out a policy, a task which should never have devolved upon it." Linderman, 188. n. 83

[292] Dawes, 153. Entry for April 11, 1898.

[293] Gould, 86.

which Congress took the nation into war."[294] This was only half-true; McKinley succeeded because McKinley on April 11 reiterated his precursor of March 17. It was Proctor who impressed the country with a Cuban question that was essentially simple and basically moral. Political, economic or military issues were secondary, even insignificant, as Proctor had it. After Proctor, neither recognition of the insurgents nor annexation of Cuba was on most Americans' minds. Instead, humanitarian sentiments moved Americans' hearts. It is noteworthy in this respect that packed galleries on April 11 cheered only one line of McKinley's message—that the "war in Cuba must stop."[295] On the day of McKinley's message, the Central Cuban Relief Committee received $ 3,500 in contributions. At that time a thousand tons of food and supplies in New York, with more trainloads *en route*,[296] were earmarked for Cuba.

Perhaps predictably, McKinley remained a fan of the Red Cross. But, actually astonishingly, charitable relief was probably the original bottom line of McKinley's "war message," meaning that in its first draft it was no war message at all. The matter is not free from doubt because evidence is scarce. That is, successive drafts of the "war message" did not survive. Cortelyou's diary is the only surviving evidence of McKinley's writing and rewriting. Cortelyou documented an editorial decision that McKinley made. On April 9, 1898, i.e., after Proctor's letter of advice, Cortelyou reported in his diary what he called the only change McKinley made in his original March 28 draft. It was "a few words to improve its historical features and *the addition of a final paragraph leaving the question in the hands of Congress*."[297] (*emphasis added*)

---

[294] Id.

[295] *New York Times*, Aptil 12, 1898, 3.

[296] Id.

[297] Cortelyou, LC, April 9, 1898.

Translating what Cortelyou called the "historical features" is easy. McKinley had to complete the history he had tracked. McKinley updated Congress on steps taken by the Spanish government after March 28, including its proclamation of a unilateral armistice. Much more difficult to interpret is the nature of the other modification. That is, Cortelyou's diary clearly implied that the "final paragraph leaving the question in the hands of Congress" was tacked on as the *new ending* of McKinley's message. What had been his last word to Congress—his request for funds to feed the starving *reconcentrados*—was obscured by a new invitation. What had been a call to support food for peace with Federal funds turned into a license for Congress to do whatever it thought best. McKinley's original message had highlighted the food for peace plan he had initiated on December 24, 1897. Congress ignored McKinley's buried request for funds for that ongoing project and solely took up his new open final paragraph to declare war.[298]

The country's final approach to war in early 1898 consisted of three acts. Movement to the point of no return began when Proctor spoke on March 17, which generated national unity in favor of military intervention. Within two weeks came the climax. The climax was McKinley's decision to accept Proctor's advice to invite Congress to decide war and peace. As a direct consequence, his request for further funding of his Red Cross peace plan became nominal. With his old peace plan reduced to the penultimate paragraph of his message, it was noticed neither

[298] Tone, 243-245. The post-April 11 sequence began with an April 19 joint resolution for Spain to leave Cuba, signed by the President April 20, the same day he sent an ultimatum to Spain to depart from Cuba or face American military intervention. On April 25 McKinley asked that Congress declare war, which it did, effective retroactively from April 21 to legitimize the American naval blockade of Cuba (April 22).

then by Congress nor thereafter by historians. The denouement followed smoothly as 10,000 people gathered at the Capitol, packing the galleries of both houses of Congress and filling the streets, on April 11. McKinley's revised message echoed Proctor's themes, prioritized the cause of humanity, and McKinley released the Cuban consular correspondences and a popular movement surged to engage the attention of a Congress open to suggestions.

The controversy over Proctor's role is hardly over. Recently, the historian whose research vindicates Proctor more than the work of any other scholar, John Lawrence Tone, in his War and Genocide in Cuba, 1895-1898, wrote off Proctor. Tone wrote that "Proctor's report helped provide one solid push for the United States to declare war, but it was based on nothing solid."[299] Tone's conclusions nonetheless mirror Proctor's conclusions. Tone assessed the bulk of evidence to be "overwhelming that the Cuban insurgency was in a nearly terminal condition by 1897 and had no chance of victory without outside help."[300] Proctor had declared the state of the civil war to be one of stalemate. Like

[299] John Lawrence Tone, War and Genocide in Cuba, 1895-1898 (Chapel Hill: The University of North Carolina Press, 2006), 210.

[300] Id., xii. Tone acknowledged that Cuban scholars have uniformly maintained that the insurgents' success was inevitable. (Pérez cites on this point Ibarra, Ideología mambisa, Botifoll, Forjadores de la concencia nacional cubana, Opatrn'y, Antecedents históricos, Bosch, De Cristóbal Colón a Fidel Castro. American public opinion in 1898 mirrored this Cuban opinion. "The condition of the Cuban campaign in 1898 . . . that the Cuban cause had stalled if it was not altogether hopeless (was) exactly the opposite of the views that had prevailed during the early months of 1898." Id., 52, which cited Chambers, Freidel, Karp, Lens, Campbell, Thomas, Brinkley and Collin on the hopelessness of the Cuban cause. Historian Foster Rhea Dulles felt that "neither side could prevail," as did others of the stalemate persuasion, Shaw and Morgan. "Conspicuously absent from most accounts of 1898 has been the possibility of U.S. intervention as a response to the imminence of a Cuban triumph." Id., 79.)

Proctor, who found in the concentration camps of Cuba a new horror for humanity to deal with, Tone characterized the vicious Cuban civil war as "the war in which the concentration camp was invented."[301] In these ways, Tone belatedly proved Proctor's case. Proctor was both an eyewitness and a canny fact-gatherer who balanced compassion for suffering Cuban civilians against antipathy to ragtag rebels who occupied rural areas but who had never taken any of Cuba's coastal cities. That is, Proctor saw or at worst intuited what Tone later substantiated from archives, a military stalemate. Tone's research reinforces the validity of Proctor's themes. Although Tone dismissed the one contemporary messenger of Cuban genocide, Redfield Proctor, as one more "jingo,"[302] Proctor spoke the demonstrable truth.

Proctor shaped the Cuban question as a compelling moral issue. Proctor was Peter the Hermit behind aroused crusaders, crusaders later depicted by his well-informed contemporary, Lyman Abbott. Professor McCartney's recent review of primary sources likewise dated the imminent approach of war from Proctor's speech. After Proctor, at least without a stand-alone bottom-line McKinley request to prop up the Red Cross in Cuba with a Treasury bailout, Cuban relief was dead. Invited to its own devices, Congress was left influenced directly by a Proctor-aroused America. Congress declared war on Spain two weeks after McKinley's Proctor-mimicking, Proctor-modified April 11 message and the simultaneous release of the Cuban consular correspondences.

---

[301] Id., xiii.

[302] Id., 243. Tone lists Proctor with four others as "the powerful party of jingoes . . . who had been pushing for war for years."

Chapter 9

CONNECTING THE DOTS

ANY CONSIDERATION OF PROCTOR'S ROLE in beginning the War of 1898 must take into account both his Senate speech and his advice to President McKinley. His low-keyed speech and his confidential advice *together* shaped American priorities not just in Washington but in the country at large. Through his speech and his advice, the Cuban question became first of all an urgent moral issue and, with the Red Cross inadequate to respond to unmet needs that were only increasing by the day, military intervention reasonably appeared to be a humanitarian necessity. On the day he delivered his report, Proctor was seen in the light of one serving man and God. People connected the dots to set sailors and soldiers in motion.

Contemporary documentation of this point is a surviving note that fellow Senator Chandler wrote Proctor at the time:

> If you ever served God and Man acceptably(,) you did so when you went to Cuba & came back & delivered your testimony in open Senate. Now(,) please see that our Senate Committee proposes something. You know the President will not recommend affirmative action of any value. $ 500,000! Oh(,) Oh.

> We should intervene and send relief by our sailors & soldiers as we would rescue a beleaguered army of 400,000 men . . . [303]

Ironically, instigating war or toppling colonial empires was not a role that Proctor ever sought. He never woke up in the morning to be a rebel. He was as conservative a man as any Republican could be, from a state not known for effusive or demonstrative emotions. As it was, Proctor made no fiery speech and the impact of his report may have surprised him by its intensity. As has been demonstrated, Proctor went to Cuba basically because a persistent correspondent and constituent, retired diplomat Paul Brooks of Rutland, Vermont kept at Proctor to see Cuba. Proctor was unlikely to have sought out what he saw—what he saw in Cuba he saw because of Clara Barton, the American Red Cross President, at whose fortuitous invitation and guided in her company Proctor saw the *reconcentrados* living in, and dying in, the world's first "concentration camps." This horror Proctor, for all of his conservatism, could not keep to himself. As Proctor returned to Washington, he sketched notes originally intended as a press release. Assistant Secretary of State William Rufus Day inscrutably suggested that audience-shy Proctor compose an address for the Senate. Then, for obvious reasons, pro-interventionist Senator William Frye of Maine, apprised of the report, immediately shepherded Proctor to speak without delay, and using only and exactly his simple but graphic handwritten notes. Brooks, Barton, Day and Frye in an impromptu procession led Proctor to rise to address the Senate on Cuba on March 17,

---

[303] Letter from W.E. Chandler to Redfield Proctor, dated March 28, 1898. It is on Senate stationery, handwritten at top "Private." Redfield Proctor Scrapbook Collection, Vermont Historical Society, Barre, Vermont, courtesy Assistant Librarian Marjorie Strong.

1898. Of course, he addressed not only his fellow Senators but the country. Gentlemen of the press scribbled notes hurriedly as Proctor spoke. They wanted something about Cuba and Proctor provided it. At that time of McKinley's ongoing and ostentatious diplomatic silence and the country's agonized wait for a report from the Navy on the *Maine*, editors pushed for copy about Cuba. Thus, Proctor's report was a godsend. Cuban-news-starved reporters in the galleries insured the broadest possible and the most immediate front-page distribution of what Chandler aptly dubbed Proctor's "testimony."

Trask called the Cuban situation in early 1898 "a full-blown rationale for intervention based on 'undiluted humanitarianism'"[304] but the rationale lacked an objective messenger. Shrill, exaggerated and profitable newspaper accounts were too many and too good to be true. People wanted someone trustworthy and unassociated with the Junta or the press to appear and tell them about Cuba. For the role of Cuban messenger, the tall, bearded Yankee who looked like Lincoln and acted as independently as a Biblical prophet, returned as one from the wilderness ready to swear that the Red Cross at its most efficient could not save Cuba. That was the news he brought, that was the story the press ran. The peaceful solution was not viable. What then? To preserve his role as objective witness, a messenger may only report and Proctor was just the messenger. Proctor left it to the people to make the logical deduction that military action could save the same people whom the Red Cross could not. Trask, noting that Proctor "made no recommendations," rightly added that "his speech certainly influenced many moderates to adopt a more bellicose view—and they were just those people who hitherto had followed the President's lead in supporting efforts to find a peaceful solution."[305]

---

[304] Trask, 36.

[305] Id.

Armed intervention went from being possible to being the only practical means of rescuing desperate sufferers on the nearby island of Cuba. Proctor spelled the end of McKinley's officially endorsed Red Cross relief effort.

Triggered by Proctor's speech on Cuba, the effort to rescue Cubans off-shore did much more, terminated the Spanish empire and made the United States a global power. But that is another story. This book is the story of how America came to bear arms in 1898 and fight against Spain. The premise of this thesis remains that Proctor's omission from or obscurity in telling the story of the origins of the War of 1898 is historically wrong. Proctor spoke and the country listened. Framing the causes of the war as an expansionist's dream is simple-minded rationalizing the origin retroactively from the result. It is anachronism. Proctor's idealistic sermon, literally read as a sermon by the iconic evangelist Dwight Moody, once spoke to and moved the heart of America. The incomparable intensity of his influence, widely recognized at the time, deserves continued recognition. Charles G. Dawes, later Vice President of the United States, wrote in his 1898 journal after another senator (Thurston) spoke, "Thurston's speech on Cuba . . . was dramatic, but will not have the effect upon the country of Senator Proctor's speech."[306] Neither the incendiary yellow press nor the fiery speeches made war. A Beacon Hill gentleman, Edwin D. Mead, independently offered that same comparison as Dawes. The Bostonian wrote Secretary of Navy

[306] Dawes, 148. Entry for March 25, 1898. Thurston's effort was spectacular. According to Russell, 448, Thurston described dreadful scenes he had seen in Cuba, declared for intervention and approaching "the close of his speech he broke down under excitement, sympathy, and sorrow, and as he sat down he bowed his head upon his desk and wept, and the galleries broke into applause that for the first time in the United States Senate was allowed to go on unchecked."

John Long[307] that "Senator Proctor's speech moved everybody profoundly—the speech of a man not loving war, but loving peace, but loving truth and duty more than peace,"[308] while "Thurston's[309] and Gallinger's melodramas are without effect here."[310]

Implicitly accepting war as necessary, Proctor simultaneously (and accurately) left no doubt about the likelihood of success. Proctor's military expertise separated him from other speechmakers in Congress. People as well as editors felt that Proctor would have warned America away from war if he had any concern that, outnumbered as its volunteers would be, or facing a larger fleet would have been dangerous folly. They thought the Proctor knew even how long the war would last. As war began, the press pressed Proctor for his predictions. To a Vermont editor on April 27, 1898, Proctor replied, "I am not a prophet, nor the son of a prophet, and I dislike to express an opinion about the length of the war." He then confided, not for publication at the time, that "our nearness to the scene of hostilities and Spain's distance, and our

---

[307] John Long, former Governor of Massachusetts, served as McKinley's Secretary of Navy, overseeing Theodore Roosevelt. His papers are largely at the Massachusetts Historical Society. His memoirs were published. Gardner Weld Allen, ed., Papers of John Davis Long, 1897-1904 (Boston: Massachusetts Historical Society, 1939).

[308] Id.

[309] Senator Thurston (Nebraska), along with Senator Gallinger (New Hampshire), and Representatives Commings (New York) and W.A. Smith (Michigan) had accepted transportation to Havana in the yacht "Anita," owned by the New York Journal. They arrived after Proctor and stayed a shorter time, making no extensive trips outside Havana. Before their speeches, the group had written articles published by the *Journal* beginning March 13, 1898, with Mrs. Thurston's open letter to "the mothers of America." (Mrs. Thurston died during the trip.) Wilkerson, n. 30, 110.

[310] Gardner Weld Allen, ed., Papers of John Davis Long, 1897-1904, (Boston: Massachusetts Historical Society, 1939), 80. Letter dated March 31, 1898.

great superiority in resources and men, ought to give us an easy victory if we manage well."[311] His March 17 speech is obviously not misunderstood to suggest the same point by implication.

As McKinley's loyal friend and reliable political ally, as a fond friend of Clara Barton, Proctor probably regretted not only that the Red Cross plan could not save the *reconcentrados* but also that it became his moral duty to announce and to vouch personally for the *bona fides* of that unpleasant deduction. At the end of his speech, by promising the country that McKinley would provide a prescription, he implied a *new* prescription. Thus it was that Proctor, of all people, an insider frequently accommodated by McKinley in patronage matters, comfortable and close to the President, who drew close attention to the President's silence. Proctor's March 17 speech did not ingratiate him with McKinley. He put the ball squarely in McKinley's court. It must be assumed that Proctor, no political novice, knew all of this. Proctor's concern about the *reconcentrados*, as he was afire inside himself with urgency for the sake of suffering humanity, freshly back from his tour of Cuba, outweighed all politics. He understood the risk of alienating the President but he took it.

A quick half-step retreat within a couple of weeks did not help his relations with McKinley. Proctor had said, and could not unsay, that McKinley would prescribe a solution. But at the White House shortly after his speech he must have divined that McKinley's reluctance to issue any prescription was intransigent. Accordingly, Proctor joined him and by follow-up letter suggested that McKinley expressly and publicly take the position that everything was up to Congress. This was ironic advice from the herald of McKinley's prescription. However, in his confidential March 29 letter, Proctor told McKinley, "If you say nothing about

[311] PFPL, Box 8, Folder 38, 357. The newspaper was the Burlington *Free Press.*

recognition or intervention, merely say that Spanish sovereignty must cease (possibly that the Cuban people be free) & leave the methods to Congress any difference about these will not affect you or your control of the situation."

That half-step back from the brink of a prescription was too little too late.

Proctor himself spoke sparingly, and only a decade later, of the argument that followed between McKinley and himself. Proctor by bland generality at first insisted in a mellow 1908 interview that their relations never changed. That may be so if one only means that Proctor continued to see and to speak his mind to the President, and vice-versa. But receptivity and content or the extent of their overlapping views certainly changed. Close friends were no longer so close. McKinley took umbrage over Proctor's timing. McKinley stormed that Proctor spoke more quickly than Proctor had implied. The nuances of friendship, the extraordinary courtesies shown disappeared. Proctor had been one of President McKinley's closest confidants, not only having a private reviewing stand on Inauguration Day but also constant and easy access to the White House. McKinley had literally stayed at Proctor's home. For one day of "the days of McKinley," August 12, 1897, Proctor's mansion in Proctor, Vermont had been the summer White House.[312] Proctor's patronage appointments from McKinley through the spring of 1898, a long list led by Admiral Dewey and Theodore Roosevelt, was second to no other politician. McKinley's neighbor and Assistant Secretary of State

[312] McKinley made a short "family values" speech from Proctor's front porch. He told the crowd that he was glad to see not only men and women but also "the many boys and girls of Proctor. There is in it all the suggestion of the family, where virtue prevails." William McKinley, Speeches and Addresses of William McKinley, From March 1, 1897 to May 30, 1900, (New York: Doubleday & McClure Co., 1900).

Day, it may be recalled, faultlessly introduced Proctor in writing to Consul Lee as "one of the closest friends of the President."[313]

This changed. While never on an "enemies' list," as the War of 1898 came and went, Proctor found formerly open doors now closed to him. Linderman chronicled the descent. Proctor needed Secretary of War Alger's appeal to be part of the Presidential party welcoming home the troops in September, 1898. Patronage requests deteriorated into futile motions and moans. By November and December, 1898 Proctor documents apologies to office-seekers, disclaiming power to obtain anything. The man whom the nation once imagined to speak for the President no longer even had the President's ear.

In early February, 1899, Proctor obviously hoped that his loyal friend, Secretary of War Alger, might run interference and have McKinley reconsider. Proctor wrote mournfully to Alger, lamenting that McKinley had "no use for my services or opinions on any matter."[314] The former advisor awaited recall that never came.

In sum, Proctor, who appears nowhere in John F. Kennedy's Profiles in Courage, was brave to make the speech he did at the time he did. He must have been conscious that his fealty to the suffering would disturb McKinley's tranquility. But, as if bitten by a Junto bug in Cuba, Proctor out-Cubaned Paul Brooks. Proctor wrote to McKinley on May 2, 1898 just after news of Admiral Dewey's victory over the Spanish fleet at Manila Bay, beginning with the understatement, "I feel well this morning." Proctor then reminded the President of "the starving poor" in Cuba. He foresaw that an

313 Linderman, 46.

314 Linderman, 53-54. In a 1908 interview, Proctor declined to reconstruct any period of soured relations. When the *Washington Post* reporter began to ask, Proctor interrupted his question about his relations with McKinley and insisted that they "remained unchanged until the day of his death."

expedited landing of American forces, linking up with General Gomez, would save thousands of American as well as Cuban lives and "clean the Spaniards out of Cuba" by July 1. In apparent frustration or imagining opposition, Proctor invoked the H word. Hearkening back to his speech, his advice letter and McKinley's echo of humanitarian duty, injecting a dose of intemperance, Proctor berated McKinley that "(i)f this is a war for humanity, as well as for Cuban freedom, this course is demanded."[315]

By rights, McKinley ought to have forgiven Proctor, who did him much good and whose compassionate heart was certainly in the right place. The uniformly favorable reaction to Proctor, mistaken as McKinley's spokesman, was political gold. It may have piqued his author's pride but Proctor's morally imperative, fact-studded sermon was a model that McKinley himself could—and did—copy. McKinley recycled Proctor's themes and placed humanitarian concerns at the top of four reasons to intervene. He offered facts about conditions in Cuba through the Cuban consular correspondences. It may be argued that because he copied Proctor and took Proctor's advice McKinley secured his drifting political base nationally, lost during his several months of silence. Contemporary accounts of both Cortelyou and Dawes demonstrate this. By taking his position behind beachheads already secured by Proctor, McKinley reclaimed his leadership of the country. Only . . . McKinley chose not to see it that way.

McKinley's dilemma is our own. Figuring out Proctor's place in our history means figuring out his place in our own lives. Perhaps surprisingly, the attention of any historian in search of the founding father of major American overseas military operations must be invited to a Vermont-born, little-traveled, English-speaking now-obscure senator, in his time the chairman

[315] Proctor to McKinley, May 2, 1898, Folder 39, 57, PFPL.

of the agricultural and forestry committee.[316] The international chapter of American history in which we still live, a willingness to bleed in the defense of the citizens of other countries who suffer oppression, militant humanitarianism, can arguably be traced back to a half-hour on March 17, 1898 when Senator Proctor came back and reported to the Senate in monotone from notes about his own ten-day trip to Cuba.

By offering the *Maine* as the cause of the War of 1898 historians unwittingly masked a war begun to rescue foreigners from their oppressors in the name of humanity. Certainly, before 1898, before Proctor, extra-territorial wars were fought in defense of American lives and property. But uniquely, literally and figuratively, the War of 1898 was the continuation of a Red Cross rescue by military means. It is historical fact that a conservative man of business rose and spoke more effectively than anyone else in Congress in behalf of Cuban *reconcentrados* and, albeit implicitly, pled for their liberation by force. Proctor's courageous act certified militant humanitarianism's respectability to churches, to Wall Street, to the country at large, and simultaneously, weirdly, as a side-effect, made him a pariah and White House "outsider."

Judging from a private letter from August 1898, written as the war was winding down, Proctor's humanitarian focus markedly diminished as his pragmatism rose. Secretary of War Alger asked how Proctor liked "his" war. Alger presumably thought that

---

[316] That is, the author of this thesis so argues. The most recent historian of humanitarian intervention did not include any reference to Proctor. Gary J. Bass, Freedom's Battle, The Origins of Humanitarian Intervention (New York: Alfred A. Knopf, 2008), wrote a book about humanitarian intervention in Greece 1820-27, in Syria in 1860, in Bulgaria in 1876, and in Armenia in 1915, to counter media suggestions that Kosovo was "the first purely humanitarian war." Id, 13. McKinley appears in a one-liner, "In 1898 (McKinley) asked Congress for permission to go to war in the 'cause of humanity.'" Id., 317.

Proctor's answer could go either way. After all, the result of the war was not the rescue of starving Cubans. Proctor was a prophet fully entitled to bless or to curse the current moment.

Proctor replied in good humor and said of the war that Alger might "call it mine, if you will." Victories at sea by Vermont's own Admiral Dewey, whom Proctor had assisted into command of the Pacific fleet, and heroic exploits of the Rough Riders led by Theodore Roosevelt, whom Proctor had recommended for Assistant Secretary of the Navy, had massed new territories for America to govern. Far beyond the *reconcentrado* goal he had espoused, the old veteran and former Secretary of War basked vicariously in his letter. Proctor told Alger in a concise but jubilant phrase that "the results are grand."

In the beginning, the War of 1898 was Proctor's speech. After the one speech, after the war, Proctor silenced himself publicly. If he saw any gap between his call to save the *reconcentrados* and the squall of the new-born American colossus, he chose to say nothing about it. Proctor's colleague, Senator Lodge, pointedly included Proctor's picture but no text in his history of the war. Proctor sat in the Senate for another decade as though he literally lost his voice.

Accordingly, only Proctor's Cuban speech, almost exactly a decade past when he died, was poignantly recalled at his memorial service in the Congregational Church in Rutland, Vermont, on Sunday evening, March 15, 1908, as several speakers spoke on various aspects of his life. R.A. Lawrence, who spoke first, naturally evoked "Redfield Proctor—The Vermonter." After Lawrence, with no surprise, Thomas W. Moloney, the speaker on Proctor as a Senator, mentioned Proctor's speech. He said that it was heard by the nation and that it had started a "war for humanity."[317] The

[317] News clipping, PFPL, n.d., but apparently a local newspaper, probably the Rutland daily.

last speaker, C.T. Fairfield, was to address "Redfield Proctor—as a Philanthropist." After Fairfield recounted how Proctor gave liberally to every worthy object, and had founded or funded many life-enhancing activities, especially in Vermont, Fairfield also predicted "the one act which will live the longest in history will be his speech in behalf of Cuba."[318] Fairfield's reference concluded the memorial speeches. Then, the congregation sang "America," a benediction was pronounced and "'Taps' was sounded by the cornet."[319] Members of the Grand Army of the Republic and of the United Spanish War Veterans,[320] Proctor's family, friends, neighbors, and employees of the Vermont Marble Company, slowly filed out of the church into the spring air of Rutland. Those who left the church may have little realized how improbable it was that Proctor gave that Cuban speech. And maybe none outside of his family knew or suspected that his words caused a division between Proctor and McKinley.

By 1908 much of the context of the Cuban speech was lost or faded in memory. But neither the crowd in Rutland that night nor modern-day historians today fail to connect the dots of Redfield Proctor's quiet words to the War of 1898, in the beginning.

---

[318] Id.

[319] PFPL, news clipping, n.d.

[320] Id. The reporter estimated that 1500 persons attended and noted that delegations from the Grand Army of the Republic, United Spanish War Veterans and Daughters of the American Revolution were "assigned special seats," presumably in the front pews.

Appendix

SCHEMATIC COMPARISON OF PROCTOR'S MARCH 17, 1898 "SPEECH" AND McKINLEY'S APRIL 11, 1898 MESSAGE TO CONGRESS

ISSUE	PROCTOR 3/17	McKINLEY 4/11
1) CUBA IS AMERICA'S CONCERN	YES	YES

Proctor said that he spoke "on account of the public interest in all that concerns Cuba," without specific reasons for any connection between the United States and Cuba.

McKinley said that he addressed Congress "because of the intimate connection of the Cuban question with the state of our own Union" and, at another point argued from Cuba's proximity, "It is no answer to say this is all in another country, belonging to another nation, and is therefore none of our business. It is specially our duty, for it is right at our door."

ISSUE	PROCTOR 3/17	McKINLEY 4/11
2) CUBAN HOLOCAUST	YES	YES

Proctor depicted Spanish soldiers' rifles as aimed "to keep in the poor *reconcentrado* women and children," and said that "deaths in the streets have not been uncommon" in these places of "foul earth, foul air, foul water and foul food or none." Reconcentration into forts meant mass death of Cubans. He came to believe that "out of a population of 1,600,000, two hundred thousand had died within these Spanish forts."

McKinley saw unfortunates in Cuba as "for the most part women and children, with aged and helpless men, enfeebled by disease and hunger" and reconcentration being "not civilized warfare (but) extermination." In the most dramatic line of his message, he declared, "In the name of humanity, in the name of civilization, in behalf of endangered American interests which give us the right and the duty to speak and to act, the war in Cuba must stop." The first of McKinley's four grounds for intervention was "to put an end to the barbarities, bloodshed, starvation, and horrible miseries now existing (in Cuba), and which the parties to the conflict are either unable or unwilling to stop or mitigate."

3) SPANISH SOVEREIGNTY DOOMED YES YES (?)

Proctor said that it is "practically the entire Cuban population on one side and the Spanish army and Spanish citizens on the other" and spoke of "the spectacle of a million and a half of people, the entire native population of Cuba, struggling for freedom and deliverance from the worst misgovernment of which (he) ever had knowledge," as Cubans he described as "businessmen who wanted peace" told him that it was "too late for peace under Spanish sovereignty."

McKinley foresaw "the enforced pacification of Cuba" but nonetheless never expressly stated that Spain could not retain vestigial authority. (Cuban peace via Cuban autonomy with loose Spanish ties had long been McKinley's quest.) However, a Cuba free of most Spanish authority was definitely clear and the end of all Spanish authority was not inconsistent with McKinley's message.

4) MILITARY SITUATION STALEMATE YES YES

Proctor said of Cuba's condition that it was "not peace nor is it war. It is desolation and distress, misery and starvation." He specified weaknesses in the Spanish army such as an undrilled, poorly-supplied force without an effective cavalry or much apparent artillery, an original 200,000 reduced to 60,000 due to death and disease.

McKinley described the military situation as "a dogged struggle," that "short of subjugation or extermination a final military victory for either side seems impracticable" and in the alternative "physical exhaustion of one or the other party, or perhaps both."

5) NO ANNEXATION OF CUBA YES YES

Proctor explicitly said, "I am not in favor of annexation."

McKinley implicitly excluded annexation, proposing the use of force only to end hostilities "and to secure in the island the establishment of a stable government."

6) RECOGNITION OF INSURGENTS (NO?) (NO?)

Proctor was diffident about meeting any insurgents on the basis of etiquette, as he had accepted the hospitality of the autonomous government. ("Having called on Governor and Captain-General Blanco and received his courteous call in return, I could not with propriety seek communication with the insurgents.")

McKinley said expressly that he did not "think it would be wise or prudent for this Government to recognize *at the present time* the independence of the so-called Cuban Republic." *(emphasis supplied)*

7) PRESIDENT SHOULD LEAD YES NO

Proctor deferred to McKinley. He said, "I merely speak of the symptoms as I saw them, but do not undertake to prescribe. Such remedial steps as may be required may safely be left to an American President and the American people."

McKinley deferred to Congress. He concluded by saying, "The issue is now with Congress. It is a solemn responsibility . . . to relieve the intolerable condition of affairs which is at our doors," their duty because, as he narrated, the efforts of the Executive Branch had produced no diplomatic solution.

8) SPECIFIC PROGRAM NO NO

Proctor declined to "prescribe" anything to the President and people.

McKinley asked Congress "to authorize and empower the President to take measures to secure a full and final termination of hostilities . . . and to use the military and naval forces of the United States as may be necessary . . ." without excluding further diplomatic effort.

9) TIME LIMITS NONE NONE

Proctor proposed none.

McKinley proposed none. This differed from 1897 diplomatic exchanges with Spain, during which he had given Spain both ultimatum-like warnings and specific deadlines.

10) MAINE AS A THEME NO NO

Proctor, speaking before the naval board's report, referred to the *Maine* only to state that he had not and would not be addressing the cause of its loss. He said, "Let us calmly wait for the report."

McKinley, writing after the report, remarkably referred only briefly to the *Maine* as an example of "elements of danger and disorder," given that "the Spanish government can not assure safety and security to a vessel of the American Navy in the harbor of Havana on a mission of peace, and rightfully there."

11) AMERICAN LIVES AND PROPERTY NO YES

Proctor makes no reference to any loss or jeopardy of American lives and property.

McKinley referred in passing to "endangered American interests which give us the right and the duty to speak and to act." He also said, "Our trade has suffered; the capital invested by our citizens in Cuba has been largely lost." More formally, among his four grounds for intervention, after the rescue of Cubans in distress, "Second. We owe it to our citizens in Cuba to afford them that protection and indemnity for life and property which no government there can or will afford . . . Third. The right to intervene may be justified by the very serious injury to the commerce, trade, and business of our people . . . Fourth, and which is of the utmost importance . . . a constant menace to our peace . . . an enormous expense." However, this latter relates back to the plight of the *reconcentrados*, the sole constant tinderbox issue.

CHRONOLOGY

1895

February 24	Cuban war for independence from Spain commences; it continues until the Spanish-American War
June 12	President Cleveland issues a proclamation of neutrality on Cuban civil war

1896

February 17	General Valeriano Weyler y Nicolau, during his first week in command of Spanish forces in Cuba, issues his infamous *reconcentrado* orders under which rural areas were depopulated as civilians were concentrated in fortified towns
December 5	President Cleveland, during his final message to Congress, warns Spain that American patience is not unlimited

1897

March 4	William McKinley is sworn in as President of the United States
April 23	William Rufus Day is sworn in as Assistant Secretary of State
August 8	Spanish "hard line" Prime Minister Cánovas is assassinated
September 9	A liberal "pragmatic" government is installed under Prime Minister Sagasta

September 13	Columbia Professor John Bassett Moore replies to Assistant Secretary of State Day's question, that the President and not the Congress possesses the power to decide whether to intervene in Cuba; when Day becomes Secretary of State in 1898, he makes Moore the Assistant Secretary of State
October 31	Weyler is recalled to Madrid
November 27	Decree from Madrid creates an autonomous Cuban government

1898

January 1	An autonomous Cuban constitution goes into effect with a limited "home rule" government under Governor-General Rámon Blanco
January 12	Anti-autonomy rioting in Havana by Spanish Cubans, including some Spanish soldiers; Second Assistant Secretary of State Alvey A. Adee advises Day that the Navy should be prepared for any emergency
January 14	Unsigned memo to President from State Department advises McKinley that the United States should recognize Cuban independence, intervening with force to oust Spain from Cuba, if force is necessary; Day (10 a.m.) tells the Spanish minister in Washington, de Lôma, that McKinley would be sending naval vessels on friendly visits to Cuba; by noon, after a meeting of Day, McKinley and two or three others at the White House (Secretary of Navy, Associate Justice McKenna of Supreme Court and possible Commanding General of the Army), McKinley decides that the battleship *Maine* should go to Havana; Day asked de Lôme to see him again and, that afternoon, tells him that the President has dispatched the *Maine* to Cuba

January 15	The *Maine*, at anchor in Key West, awaits arrival of the North Atlantic Squadron
January 16	The squadron departs from Hampton Roads, Virginia
January 17	Dawes in his journal reports "many callers" upon McKinley this day, naming five senators including Proctor
January 23	The squadron arrives at Key West
January 24	The squadron, now including the *Maine*, steams to Dry Tortugas, from which the *Maine* separates at 11 p.m.
January 25	The *Maine* drops anchor in Havana
January 27	Annual diplomatic dinner at the White House
February 6	Proctor writes "less than even" likelihood of his going to Cuba; Clara Barton leaves Washington for Cuba with J.K. Elwell, Spanish-speaking shipping magnate from Ohio, resident in Santiago for six years
February 9	American newspapers publish copies of a private letter of de Lôme criticizing McKinley as weak and the Cuban autonomy program as a sham; Clara Barton and Elwell reach Havana
February 14	Proctor requests letters of recommendation to Cuban businessmen
February 15	Proctor "doubts very much" he will visit Cuba; the *Maine* explodes
February 17	A naval board of inquiry is established under Admiral Sampson; Proctor writes that he may visit Cuba "if not at war"
February 21	Proctor leaves Washington for Florida, "possibly Cuba"; the Sampson board begins its closed-door proceedings
February 19-25	Proctor fishes in Florida with Colonel Parker

February 25	Proctor and Parker take steamer from Key West to Havana
February 26	Proctor and Parker arrive in Havana, meet American Consul Lee, Clara Barton, Senator Frye, news reporters; during his visit of ten days (February 26-March 8) Proctor visits the four western provinces of Cuba with Barton and Red Cross staff
March 9	Proctor and Parker take steamer from Havana to Key West; both houses of Congress unanimously pass a $ 50 million national defense bill, funds to be expended in the President's sole judgment
March 13	Proctor arrives back in Washington
March 17	Proctor meets with Assistant Secretary of State Day; Proctor meets with President McKinley; Proctor runs into Senator Frye, who pushes him to give his report to the Senate immediately; he does so, reciting from notes for about a half-hour
March 17-20	Wide publicity is given to Proctor's speech
March 21	The Sampson board inquiry concludes its report
March 24	The Sampson board report arrives in Washington
March 25	President McKinley receives the report
March 28	President McKinley presents the report to Congress; however, it was already public information through a leak to the press the same morning
April 6	Originally-scheduled date for President's message to Congress; withheld until April 11 at request of Consul Lee for more time to evacuate Americans from Cuba

April 11	President McKinley asks Congress to issue an ultimatum to Spain, tantamount to a declaration of war ; the State Department releases the "Cuban Correspondences"
April 19	Congress passes a resolution implying Cuba's sovereignty
April 25	Congress declares war retroactive to April 22

(Chronology adapted and synthesized from Kenneth E. Hendrickson, Jr.'s The Spanish-American War, Elbridge Brooks's The Story of Our War with Spain and with dates from other sources, e.g., Clara Barton, The Red Cross (1898), and Chester Bowie's dissertation on Redfield Proctor.)

Bibliography

Archives

Clara Barton Papers. Library of Congress, Microfilm Division.
George Cortelyou Papers. Library of Congress, Manuscript Division.
Massachusetts Historical Society.
Proctor Papers. Proctor Free Public Library, Proctor, Vermont.

Newspapers

Boston Globe
Chicago Tribune
New York Times

Periodicals

Congressional Record
North American Review

Theses and Dissertations

Barcan, Arthur. "American Imperialism and the Spanish-American War." M.A. thesis, Columbia University, 1940.

Bowie, Chester Winston. "Redfield Proctor: A Biography." Ph.D. dissertation, University of Wisconsin, 1980.

Cooley, Roger G. "Redfield Proctor: A Study in Leadership, the Vermont Period." Ph.D. dissertation, University of Rochester, 1955.

Ford, Benjamin Temple. "A Duty to Serve: The Governmental Career of George Bruce Cortelyou." Ph.D. dissertation, Columbia University, 1963.
Tweedy, Ruth Lois. "The Life of Redfield Proctor." M.A. thesis, University of Illinois (Urbana), 1942.

Articles

Davis, Michelle Bray, and Rollin W. Quimby. "Senator Proctor's Cuban Speech: Speculations on a Cause of the Spanish-American War." *Quarterly Journal of Speech* 55 (April 1969): 131-41.
Partridge, Frank C. "Redfield Proctor, His Life and Public Services." *Proceedings of the Vermont Historical Society for the Years 1913-1914* (1915): 57-123.

Bibliographies

Venzon, Anne Cipriano. The Spanish-American War: an annotated bibliography. (New York: Garland, 1990).
______________. The Spanish-American War: a selective bibliography. (Lanham, MD: Scarecrow Press, 2003).

Books

Bacon, Donald C., Roger H. Davidson, Newton Keller, eds. The Encyclopedia of the United States Congress. 3 volumes. (New York: Simon & Schuster, 1965).
Balakian, Peter. The Burning Tigris, The Armenian Genocide and America's Response. (New York: HarperCollins Publishers, 2003.)
Barton, William E. The Life of Clara Barton, Founder of the American Red Cross. (New York: AMS Press, 1969 reprint of 1922 edition).

Bitzer, G.W. Billy Bitzer, His Story. (New York: Farrar, Straus and Giroux, 1973).

Blow, Michael. A Ship to Remember, The *Maine* and the Spanish-American War. (New York: William Morrow and Company, Inc., 1992).

Brands, H.W. The Reckless Decade, America in the 1890s. (New York: St. Martin's Press, 1995).

Brooks, Elbridge Streeter. The Story of Our War with Spain. (Boston: Lothrop Publishing Company, 1899).

Burton, David H. Clara Barton, In the Service of Humanity. (Westport, Connecticut: Greenwood Press, 1995).

Chadwick, F.E. The Relations of the United States and Spain, Diplomacy. (New York: Charles Scribner's Sons, 1909).

Chidsey, Donald Barr. The Spanish-American War, A Behind-the-Scenes Account of the War in Cuba. (New York: Crown Publishers, Inc., 1971).

Dawes, Charles G. A Journal of the McKinley Years. (Chicago: The Lakeside Press, 1950).

Dobson, John. Reticent Expansionism, The Foreign Policy of William McKinley. (Pitsburgh: Duquesne University Press, 1988).

Dunn, Arthur Wallace. From Harrison to Harding, A Personal Narrative, Covering a Third of a Century 1888-1921. (New York: Putnam's, 1922).

Foner, Eric, ed. Our Lincoln, New Perspectives on Lincoln and His World. (New York: W.W. Norton and Company, 2008).

Gilbo, Patrick F. The American Red Cross, The First Century. (New York: Harper & Row, Publishers, 1981).

Gould, Lewis L. The Modern American Presidency. (Lawrence, Kansas: University Press of Kansas, 2003).

______________. The Presidency of William McKinley. (Lawrence, Kensas: The Regents Press of Kansas, 1980).

______________. The Spanish-American War and President McKinley. (Lawrence, Kansas: University Press of Kansas, 1982).
Hendrickson, Kenneth E., Jr. The Spanish-American War. (Westport, CT: Greenwood Press, 2003).
Hoover, Irwin Hood. Forty-Two Years in the White House. (Boston: Houghton Mifflin, 1934).
Kohlsaat, H.H. From McKinley to Harding, Personal Recollections of Our Presidents. (New York: Charles Scribner's Sons, 1923).
Leech, Margaret. In the Days of McKinley. (New York: Harper & Brothers, 1959).
Linderman, Gerald F. The Mirror of War: American Society and the Spanish-American War. (Ann Arbor: University of Michigan Press, 1974).
Lodge, Henry Cabot. The War with Spain. (New York: Harper & Brothers Publishers, 1899).
McCartney, Paul. Power and Progress: American National Identity, the War of 1898, and the Rise of American Imperialism. (Baton Rouge: Louisiana State University Press, 2006).
McKinley, William. Speeches and Addresses of William McKinley, From March 1, 1897 to May 30, 1900. (New York: Doubleday & McClure Co., 1900).
McLean, Joseph Eregina. William Rufus Day, Supreme Court Justice from Ohio. (Baltimore: The Johns Hopkins Press, 1946).
Morgan, H. Wayne. America's Road to Empire, The War with Spain and Overseas Expansion. (New York: Wiley, 1965).
______________. William McKinley and His America. (New York: Syracuse University Press, 1963).
Olcott, Charles S. The Life of William McKinley. (Boston: Houghton Mifflin, 1916), 2 volumes
Offner, John L. An Unwanted War, The Diplomacy of the United States and Spain over Cuba, 1895-1898. (Chapel Hill, N.C.: The University of North Carolina Press, 1992).

O'Toole, G.J.A. The Spanish War, An American Epic—1898. (New York: W.W. Norton & Company, 1984).

Pérez, Louis A., Jr. The War of 1898, The United States and Cuba in History and Historiography. (Chapel Hill: The University of North Carolina Press, 1998).

Phillips, Kevin. William McKinley. (New York: Henry Holt and Company, 2003).

Pratt, Julius W. Expansionists of 1898: The Acquisition of Hawaii and the Spanish Islands. (Baltimore: The Johns Hopkins Press, 1936).

Pryor, Elizabeth Brown. Clara Barton, Professional Angel. (Philadelphia: University of Pennsylvania Press, 1987).

Rickover, H.G. How the Battleship *Maine* was Destroyed. (Washington, D.C.: Naval History Division, Department of the Navy, 1976).

Russell, Henry B. An Illustrated History of Our War with Spain: Its Causes, Incidents and Results. (Hartford, Connecticut: A.D. Worthington & Co., Publ., 1898).

Sigsbee, Charles D. The "Maine," An Account of her Destruction in Havana Harbor. (New York: The Century Co., 1898).

Titherington, Richard. A History of the Spanish-American War of 1898. (New York: D. Appleton, 1900).

Tone, John Lawrence. War and Genocide in Cuba, 1895-1898. (Chapel Hill: The University of North Carolina Press, 2006).

Trask, David F. The War with Spain in 1898. (New York: Macmillan Publishing Co., Inc., 1981).

Traxel, David. 1898, The Birth of the American Century. (New York: Alfred A. Knopf, 1998).

U.S. Congress. Redfield Proctor (Late a Senator from Vermont): Memorial Addresses. 60th Cong., 2d sess., 1908-1909. Washington: Government Printing Office, 1909.

Welch, Richard E., Jr. The Presidencies of Grover Cleveland. (Lawrence, Kansas: University Press of Kansas, 1988).

Wilkerson, Marcus M. Public Opinion and the Spanish-American War, A Study in War Propaganda. (New York: Russell & Russell, 1932).

Wisan, Joseph. The Cuban Crisis as reflected in the New York Press, 1895-1898. (New York: Octagon Books, 1934).

Young, Marilyn Blatt. American Expansionism, The Critical Issues. (Boston, Little, Brown and Co., 1973).

Zimmerman, Warren. First Great Triumph, How Five Americans Made Their Country a World Power. (New York: Farrar, Straus and Giroux, 2002).

Index

Page numbers with "n" indicate references to notes.

R

S